fabric PAINTING
WITH DONNA DEWBERRY

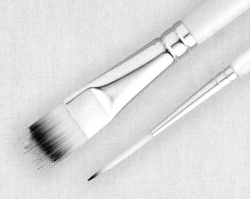

fabric PAINTING

WITH DONNA DEWBERRY

North Light Books, Cincinnati, Ohio
www.mycraftivity.com

www.fwpublications.com

Other fine North Light Books are available from your local bookstore, art supply store or online at www.mycraftivity.com.

12   11   10   09   08   5   4   3   2   1

Distributed in Canada by Fraser Direct
100 Armstrong Avenue
Georgetown, ON, Canada L7G 5S4
Tel: (905) 877-4411

Distributed in the U.K. and Europe by David & Charles
Brunel House, Newton Abbot, Devon, TQ12 4PU, England
Tel: (+44) 1626 323200, Fax: (+44) 1626 323319
Email: postmaster@davidandcharles.co.uk

Distributed in Australia by Capricorn Link
P.O. Box 704, S. Windsor NSW, 2756 Australia
Tel: (02) 4577-3555

Library of Congress Cataloging-in-Publication Data

Dewberry, Donna S.
      Fabric painting with Donna Dewberry. / Donna Dewberry.
            p. cm
      Includes index.
      ISBN 978-1-60061-073-8 (pbk. : alk. paper)
   1. Textile painting. I. Title.
TT851.D49 2008
746.6—dc22

                                                    2008002055

Edited by Kathy Kipp
Designed by Clare Finney
Production coordinated by Greg Nock
Photography by Brian Steege, Christine Polomsky,
Tim Grondin, and Ric Deliantoni.
Wardrobe styling by Monica Skrzelowski
Make-up by Cass Smith

METRIC CONVERSION CHART

TO CONVERT	TO	MULTIPLY BY
Inches	Centimeters	2.54
Centimeters	Inches	0.4
Feet	Centimeters	30.5
Centimeters	Feet	0.03
Yards	Meters	0.9
Meters	Yards	1.1

ABOUT THE AUTHOR

Donna Dewberry is the most successful and well-known decorative painter ever. Since 1998, she has created ten full-size instructional books for North Light. She is a popular television presenter on the Home Shopping Network, and her new program, "The Donna Dewberry Show," can be seen weekly on PBS stations nationwide. Her one-stroke designs are licensed for home décor and quilt fabrics, wallpapers, borders, stencils. etc. Donna's most recent North Light books are *Fast & Fun Landscape Painting* (2007) and *Donna Dewberry's Essential One-Stroke Painting Reference* (2008).

DEDICATION

This book is dedicated to my daughters, daughters-in-law and my granddaughters. They are truly wonderful and many of my inspirations for ideas come from my interactions with them. I love my time spent with them and enjoy each of their individual personalities. We always seem to have a good time and I am truly inspired by them and the talents they possess.
Love Mom, Mima

ACKNOWLEDGMENTS

I would like to give thanks to all those Decorative Painters who through the years have shared their lives with me. I draw strength each day from you and the experiences you share with me. All of you are special and your talent truly makes the world a little more beautiful each day.

Recently upon a visit to Bok Tower in Lake Wales, Florida, my husband and I reflected upon someone who is going through a difficult time. While amongst the beautiful gardens at the tower we immediately thought of her. After a few tears, we composed ourselves and shared the fact that, when the day is over, the real value we have in our lives will be in the people we have known and shared it with. All of you have enriched my life and for that I am eternally grateful.

In closing I would like to personally acknowledge Nora and thank her for allowing me to be part of her life. She is truly a wonderful person and I am better for having known her.

contents

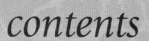

MATERIALS

Acrylic paints for fabric	8
Brushes	8
Double loading carousel	9
Electric applicator for crystals	9
Shirt form for painting on t-shirts	9
Paint color chart	10
Glitter and crystals for embellishments	11

ONE-STROKE PAINTING ON FABRICS

Double loading the brush	12
Using fabric medium	12
Multi-loading the brush	13
Using dimensional paints: do's and don'ts	14
Lacy effects with dimensional paints	15
Outlining: the right and wrong way	15
Fixing mistakes and cleaning up lines	15
One-stroke leaves and petals	16

HOW TO ADD SPARKLE AND PIZAZZ!

Using glitter paint	20
Using art glitter from a jar	20
Applying crystals with an applicator	21

40 FABULOUS HANDPAINTED DESIGNS ON FABRIC

SECTION 1: CLOTHING

Denim Jeans	24
Linen Swing Jacket	27
Watercolor Tee	30
Dressy Black Pants	33
Classic Denim Jacket	38
Tailored Shirt	40
Long A-line Skirt	42
Sparkly Camisole	44

SECTION 2: ACCESSORIES

Ballet Flats	46
Butterfly Socks	48
Dressy Clutch Purse	50
Casual Handbag	52
Elegant Evening Wrap	55
Laptop Computer Bag	57

SECTION 3: GIFTS

Wedding Album	60
Floral Photo Album	62
Christening Gown	66
Ring Bearer's Pillow	69
Baby Bibs	71
Baby Bloomers	74
Decorative Pillows	76

SECTION 4: KITCHEN

Dish Towels & Pot Holders	80
Kitchen Tablecloth	82
Elegant Tablecloth	87
Floral Napkins	92
Chef's Apron	99

SECTION 5: BED & BATH

Lined Wicker Basket	104
Monogrammed Pillowcases	106
Satin Bathrobe	110
Parson's Chair Cover	113
Bath Towels	116
Quilted Throw	120

Resources	126
Index	127

materials

3/4-inch (19mm) flat

1/2-inch (13mm) scruffy

no. 2 script liner

5/8-inch (16mm) angular

1/2-inch (13mm) feather

no. 10 filbert

ACRYLIC PAINTS FOR FABRIC

For all the projects in this book, I used Plaid FolkArt Fabric Paints. These are brush-on colors that come in handy squeeze bottles and are available at your local art and craft supply store. They have a rich, creamy consistency that offers excellent coverage, even on dark fabrics, and they remain soft to the touch when dry—no cracking, flaking or hard spots. They are durable enough for many years of wear and are great for just about any surface, including denim, cotton, polyester/cotton blends, woven blends such as linen, and home decor textiles such as silk and rayon. FolkArt Fabric Medium is used instead of water to thin the paint, to smooth it out if you're painting on rough or textured fabrics, and to help blend your double loaded colors on your palette. FolkArt Fabric Paints also come in metallic colors to add shine to your projects, and in dimensional colors (including glitter!) to add texture and interest. I often use the dimensional paints to create elegant linework such as curls and scrolls.

BRUSHES

The standard One-Stroke Acrylic Brushes can be used for fabric painting, but for best results, I use the One-Stroke Fabric Brushes. These feature stiff white bristles that are designed specially for painting on fabrics. The bristles are tipped in green so you can spot these brushes quickly in your brush caddy.

DOUBLE LOADING CAROUSEL

To make double loading your brushes even easier, the One-Stroke Double Loading Carousel allows you to pick up just the right amount of paint on your flat brushes. It has sixteen wedge-shaped wells for your colors and a center well for your fabric medium. It comes with a sealed lid that holds a dampened sponge to keep your paints fresh and moist longer. On page 12, I show you how to double load your brush and pick up medium using the carousel.

ELECTRIC APPLICATOR FOR CRYSTALS

This is a very easy way to apply individual, preglued "hot-fix" crystals and rhinestones to your painted clothing and accessories. The applicator plugs in and the metal wand tip heats up to melt the glue on the back of the crystal just enough to affix it permanently to the fabric. The brand I use comes with eight different-sized tips so you can apply different sizes of crystals, and a little stand to keep the hot metal tip off your table. The applicator allows you to use great precision when attaching your crystals or rhinestones to your design and it keeps your hands free of any glue. See the Resources section in the back of the book for more information.

ONE-STROKE FABRIC PAINTING SHIRT FORM

To make fabric painting even easier, I designed this shirt form to use whenever you're painting on a regular t-shirt, a scoop-neck tee, camisole, cotton shirt, blouse, or any top where you want to keep the front and the neckline smooth and wrinkle-free while you paint. Slip the form between the front and back of the shirt to prevent any bleed-through of your color. Unlike cardboard forms, the sturdy, smooth polyethylene surface can be wiped clean with a damp paper towel to remove any wet paint and reused over and over.

paints & embellishments

FOLKART FABRIC PAINTS

Asphaltum   Autumn Leaves   Berry Wine   Brilliant Blue   Coastal Blue   Engine Red   Fresh Foliage

Lavender   Lemon Custard   Licorice   Light Red Oxide   Magenta   Orchid   Pure Orange

Vintage Orange   Wicker White   Yellow Citron   Yellow Light   Yellow Ochre   Hauser Green Medium   Thicket

METALLIC FABRIC PAINTS

Metallic Amethyst   Metallic Blue Topaz   Inca Gold Metallic/ Metallic Pure Gold Dimensional   Metallic Peridot/ Metallic Peridot Dimensional   Pearl Champagne Dimensional

Pearl White Dimensional   Metallic Rose Shimmer   Silver Sterling/ Metallic Silver Dimensional   Metallic Solid Bronze/ Metallic Solid Bronze Dimensional   Metallic Taupe

Glitter Blue Ocean

Glitter Gold

Glitter Silver

Glitter Ice Sparkle

GLITTER DIMENSIONAL FABRIC PAINTS

FolkArt Fabric Paints also come in several glittery colors such as these (top right) to add dimension and sparkle to your designs. Their handy squeeze bottles with a writing tip make it easy to outline your painted areas or draw stems, curlicues and scrolls. The paint comes out of the bottle white but becomes clear when it dries, leaving only the glitter showing. It remains flexible when dry and the glitter does not flake off. I've used glitter paints on several projects in this book—check out the denim jeans on page 24 and the floral photo album on page 62.

ULTRAFINE ART GLITTER

There is a big difference between craft glitter and art glitter like this. Art glitter is very fine and comes loose in small jars. It is sprinkled on over adhesive or wet paint and when dry, excess is brushed off with a soft brush. For the projects in this book, I used Ultrafine Art Glitter in some of the colors shown at right. These are from a kit of six colors called "Barnyard." See the Resources section in the back of the book for more information.

CRYSTALS

There's nothing like using fine crystals to add pizazz to your painted clothing and accessories! I used these preglued "Hot-Fix" Swarovski Rhinestones on many projects, such as the sparkly sunflower camisole on page 44 and the ballet flats on page 46. To apply them I used the electric applicator wand shown on page 9. Each crystal has a thin layer of glue already on the back so you do not have to get your fingers sticky!

Melone
Ultrafine
Transparent

Fire Engine
Ultrafine
Opaque

Ensalada
Ultrafine
Transparent

ULTRAFINE
ART
GLITTER

Fossil
Ultrafine
Transparent

Ruddy Red
Ultrafine
Transparent

Mustard
Ultrafine
Transparent

Olivine

Aurora
Borealis

CRYSTALS

Black
Diamond

Volcano

Clear
Diamond

Citrine

one-stroke painting on fabrics

DOUBLE LOADING THE BRUSH

1 Place the two colors you want to double load next to each other on the double loading carousel. Leave an empty wedge next to them. Set your brush into the two colors straddling the wedge divider so the bristles are split in half. Press down and stroke up the wedge a bit.

2 Tilt the handle toward you and pull back into the paint puddles. Here you can see the two colors loaded on the first side of the brush.

3 Move over to the empty wedge and work the paint into the bristles by stroking back and forth to blend the colors. Press down hard on the bristles to force paint into them.

USING FABRIC MEDIUM

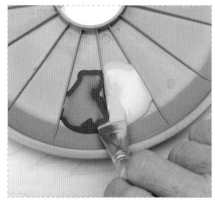

1 Place some Fabric Medium into the center circular well of the double loading carousel. Dip the tips of the bristles straight into the Fabric Medium.

2 Come back to the same blending wedge and work the medium into the brush.

3 Then pull the stroke on your fabric. Here you can clearly see the two colors double loaded on the brush. The medium helps smooth out your strokes as you move over the nap of the fabric.

MULTI-LOADING THE BRUSH

1 To achieve a variety of colors in one stroke, you can multi-load your flat brush with up to four colors. Begin by double loading your brush with your two main colors, such as the Magenta and Yellow shown above. Work these two colors into your bristles, then pick up your third color on one corner. Here I'm picking up Wicker White on the yellow side.

2 Turn the brush over and dip the corner of the Magenta side into your fourth color; here it's Berry Wine.

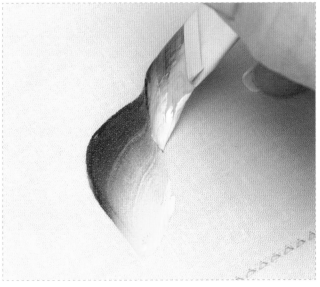

3 In an empty wedge on the double loading carousel, stroke back and forth to work the colors into your brush.

4 Pull your stroke on your fabric. You can see the four colors in this one stroke: white at the bottom edge, then yellow, then the magenta and finally the dark red. Many flower petals have gradations of color like this, so practice multi-loading your flat brush as often as you can.

1 Here are a few do's and don'ts when using dimensional paint on your fabric items. DON'T paint your line by holding the bottle straight up and DON'T jam the tip into the fabric. This produces a line with ridges and lumps.

2 DON'T hold the bottle so the tip is off the fabric. You will not be able to control your line, as the paint will fall where it wants to.

3 DO begin by touching the tip to the fabric with the bottle straight up.

4 DO tilt the bottle so you can pull it in the direction you need to go. Never push it toward you.

5 DO pull the tip in a smooth, quick movement. Keep consistent pressure on the bottle—don't squeeze and release, squeeze and release. The line will break as shown at the bottom. Keep squeezing until you've reached the end of your line.

LACY EFFECTS WITH DIMENSIONAL PAINTS

1 The secret to achieving a lacy look using dimensional paint is to always keep consistent pressure on the bottle as you squeeze out the line of paint. Don't let the line break until you get to the edge of the area you're painting. Begin by using the tip of the bottle to draw a couple of connected S-shapes.

2 Continue squeezing out the paint making a curving, looping line that looks like puzzle pieces.

3 Don't let the line break, and don't let it touch any part of the line you've been making. Lift the tip of the bottle from the garment only when you've reached the outer edge of your painted area. For an example of this lacy effect on clothing, see the collar and pocket flaps of the denim jacket on page 39.

OUTLINING: THE WRONG WAY AND THE RIGHT WAY

1 Outlining with dimensional paint adds a special touch to your designs, but it needs to be done freely and quickly. In this example of blue dragonfly wings outlined in white dimensional paint, the outlining is too tight, too close to the edges of the blue wings. And on the smaller wings, I went too slowly and the outline got fat and lumpy.

2 Here's how the outlining should be done: loose, free, almost abstractly. Unlike your elementary school drawings, you do not have to stay within the lines. It's much more attractive if the lines just follow the general shape of the painted areas.

FIXING MISTAKES AND CLEANING UP LINES

  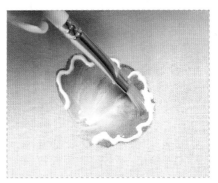

1 Sometimes you may not be happy with an outline or detail you painted using the dimensional fabric paint. In this photo you can see that the outline is a little ragged.

2 To clean up the bad area, dampen a small flat brush and scoop up the white paint. Wipe the paint off the brush on a paper towel.

3 Then clean up the line with the brush.

ONE-STROKE LEAVES

1 Double load a flat brush with a lighter green and a darker green. Start on the chisel edge. Push down on the bristles to fan them out a bit.

2 Turn the brush slightly as you stroke.

3 Lift back up to the chisel edge to form the tip of the leaf.

SINGLE-STROKE RUFFLED-EDGE LEAVES

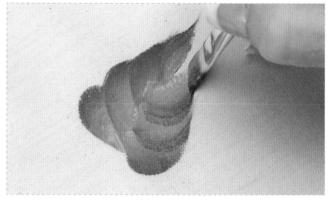

1 This leaf consists of a series of single strokes that get smaller and shorter and overlap each other slightly as they get closer to the tip. Double load a darker green and a lighter green. Start at the base and pull a stroke outward, then curve it back toward the center as you lift to the chisel edge.

2 Pull more strokes working upward toward the tip, narrowing each one and overlapping as you go. Notice how the darker green on the double-loaded brush serves to separate the segments.

3 The final stroke narrows, straightens and lifts to the chisel edge to form the tip of the leaf.

4 Pull a stem partway into the center using the chisel edge. When painting on fabric, your edges will be softer and more indistinct than when painting on paper or other hard surface. Don't go back and try to fill in the edges—you'll lose that hand-painted quality and your designs may start to look like appliqués.

LONG-TAILED COMMA STROKE

1 Double load a flat brush with a darker and a lighter green. Press down on the bristles to fan them out and form the widest part of the comma.

2 Begin pulling the stroke as you stand back up to the chisel edge.

3 Slide down, staying up on the chisel edge, to form the long skinny tail.

SCROLLING LEAF

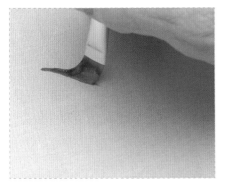  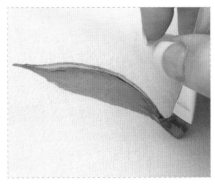

1 Double load a flat brush with a darker and a lighter green. Start the stroke on the chisel edge.

2 Press down on the bristles to widen the middle section of the leaf.

3 Stand back up to the chisel edge and pull a long curving stroke for the leaf tip.

TWO-STEP CURLS

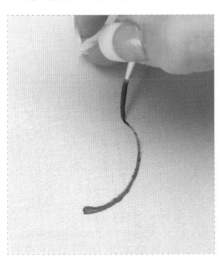 

1 Using a no. 2 script liner and inky paint, start the long part of the curl from the base and pull upward.

2 Start at the other end and paint a tight loop, then pull your line toward the first one. Connect the two lines where they meet.

ROSE LEAVES

1 Double load a flat brush with a medium green and a lighter yellow-green. Begin at the base and paint a large comma stroke that slides out, then curves back toward the center and stops.

2 Add one or two more comma strokes that get progressively smaller.

3 Finish with a straight comma stroke and lift to the chisel to form the tip of the leaf.

CUPPED ACANTHUS LEAF

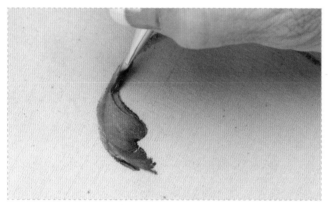 

1 Double load a large flat brush with two colors that are close in hue. Here I'm using a darker green and a lighter green. Place a curving line for the center vein. Ruffle out and slide back to the vein.

2 Continue ruffling out and sliding back, making the strokes larger to widen the center of the leaf. Notice that there are gaps between a few of the strokes—these indicate the separate segments of the leaf.

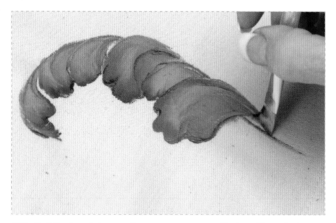 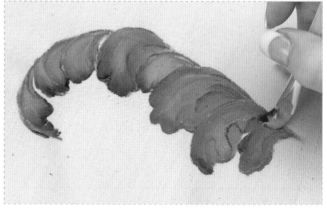

3 Roll the brush in your fingers as you move it along the vein, keeping the light green corner down.

4 Pick up more dark green on one corner of the brush and paint a wavy line to ruffle the edge. Finish with a small leaf segment at the base the same as you did in Step 1.

SCALLOP-EDGED LEAF

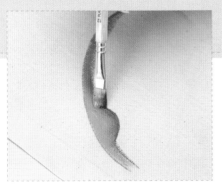

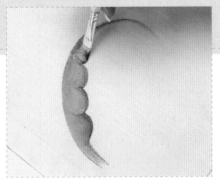

1 Double load a flat brush with two shades of green. Paint a smooth, wide, curving band for the center vein. Begin at the base and paint the first scallop.

2 Continue painting more wide scallops along the curving line of the center vein. Keep the darker green to the outside.

3 Finish with smaller and smaller scallops to form the tip end of the leaf.

SEGMENTED SEA-SHELL STROKE

1 To get better paint coverage on fabric, break up the seashell stroke into several segments that overlap. Double load a flat brush with blue and white. Start on the left side and press down on the bristles. Wiggle only the outside edge.

2 Start at the base again, overlapping the stroke you just made, and wiggle another segment of the shell shape.

3 Start at the base again, overlapping the second stroke you just made, and wiggle the final segment, sliding back to the base to finish the right side.

SERRATED-TIP PETAL

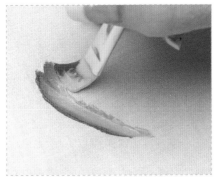

1 Double load a flat brush with red and yellow. Slide up to the tip to form the outside left edge of the petal, leading with the red side.

2 Do a short, jagged zigzag stroke at the very outer tip of the petal.

3 Slide back down to the base to form the left edge of the petal, with the red side of the brush to the outside.

USING GLITTER DIMENSIONAL PAINT

1 No matter what color you are using, all Glitter Dimensional paint comes out looking milky white. This is the glue part of the paint. The glitter is mixed into the glue but is a little hard to see at this point. As with any dimensional paint, squeeze the bottle consistently, not with a stop-and-start action, to get a smooth line with no bumps or dry spots.

2 This is how it looks when it dries after about 15-30 minutes. The milkiness is gone and only the glitter shows. Let it air dry for 24 hours to set it permanently.

APPLYING LOOSE ART GLITTER

1 The Art Glitter I'm using for the projects in this book is labeled "Ultrafine" and comes in little jars with a bottle of adhesive. Rather than use the adhesive, I just add the glitter to my wet paint, whether it is the brush-on or the dimensional. As long as the paint is wet, the glitter will adhere to it. Begin with your design in the colors of your choice. Here I'm using Lemon Custard dimensional for the yellow flower and Fresh Foliage dimensional for the leaf and curl. While the paint is still wet, sprinkle the glitter color of your choice over the wet paint using a small plastic spoon. Here, I'm sprinkling Melone Ultrafine Transparent glitter over the yellow paint.

2 For the leaf and curl, sprinkle Ensalada Ultrafine Transparent glitter over the green paint.

3 This is how the glittered design looks when it's completely dry. It's best to let it air-dry for 24 hours to guarantee that the underpaint is dry. Shake off the excess into a small bowl or pan if you want to save it, or into a trash can if you don't. (If you save the glitter, remember that your two glitter colors are now mixed together. Don't return this mix to the original jars—save it in a clean jar and label it as a mix with the names of the two original colors.) Use a large soft brush to gently brush off any glitter that has drifted onto your fabric.

1 Crystals or rhinestones can add a lovely sparkle when used on clothing. I painted brightly colored flowers on the green linen jacket shown on page 27, and decided to add crystals to some of the flower centers. I let the paint dry completely before starting to attach the crystals.

2 To enhance the colors of the jacket, I chose "Citrine" pre-glued crystals by Swarovski. On the backs of the crystals you can see the dark gray layer of glue. Place the crystals face up on a hard, flat surface such as a small ceramic plate or dish.

3 Attach the correct size of metal tip to your applicator, plug it in, and let it heat up for a minute. For this size of crystal, I'm using the 4mm tip. Gently place the tip over the face-up crystal (do not push down) and lift it off the plate.

4 This is how the crystal looks in the metal applicator tip. The pre-glued back should be facing outward. Watch for the glue to begin melting. It will look a little wet, but do not allow it to bubble.

5 Gently apply the crystal to the flower center and immediately lift the tip off. Rest the hot tip on the little stand that's included in the kit when not in use. Unplug it and let it cool completely before storing.

6 Apply as many crystals as you want, but remember, a little goes a long way. You want the painting to be the star—the crystals act as an accent, almost like putting a diamond pin on your jacket's lapel.

40 *fabulous* handpainted designs *on fabric*

Now that you've seen how easy it is to paint on fabric, let's have some fun! Pick out a pair of jeans from your closet or a dishtowel from your kitchen and try your hand at it. As you will see in the coming pages, you can paint on almost any kind of fabric, from the nubby silk of decorative pillows to the textured linen of a dressy jacket. Here are some tips to help you get started:

- Don't use water with FolkArt Fabric Paints to thin them or to make inky paint. Use only the Fabric Medium. Dip your loaded brush into the medium to help smooth your strokes over the fabric and to keep your brush from dragging.
- Dimensional Glitter Paint comes out of the bottle milky. After about 15 minutes, it will be dry enough so you can begin to see the glitter. When it is completely dry after about 24 hours, the milkiness becomes clear and you will see only the glitter.
- When using Fabric Paints, paint wet-into-wet for best blending. Don't let your colors dry before adding another. And if you are detailing your brush-on paints with dimensional paints, do it right away before the brush-on paint dries.
- With some fabrics, the paint may bleed through, especially if the fabric is thin like cotton or silk. To keep from getting the paint on the back of your clothing item, separate the front from the back with the FolkArt One-Stroke Fabric Painting Form, or use a sheet of plastic film or a flat plastic bag.
- If you are painting on a new item, I suggest you wash and dry the item first, if possible, before painting on it. This will remove any sizing in the fabric and allow it to shrink. However, please do not use liquid fabric softener in your washer or fabric softener sheets in your dryer. Fabric softener leaves a coating on fabric that prevents good adhesion of the paint. After the paint has dried completely, then you can wash and dry the item as you normally would. If you have applied crystals to your painted design, turn the item inside out when you put it in the dryer to protect the crystals.

denim jeans

MATERIALS NEEDED

Colors: Inca Gold Metallic, Licorice and Licorice Dimensional, Metallic Pure Gold Dimensional, Glitter Gold Dimensional

Brushes: no. 8 flat, 5/8-inch (16mm) angular

Surface: Denim jeans, dark blue, from Cold-water Creek. Similar jeans are available at any department or specialty store. Machine wash and dry jeans before painting to remove sizing. Do not use liquid fabric softener or fabric softener sheets in the dryer—this will prevent good adhesion of the paint.

Additional Supplies: Swarovski Hot-Fix rhinestones in Citrine color; electric applicator with 4mm tip.

1 Load Inca Gold Metallic on a 5/8-inch (16mm) angular brush. Paint large comma strokes, pushing down hard to get the wide area at the top, then pull a long tail. Vary the size and length of the comma strokes for a more interesting design.

2 Paint the lower scroll design the same way, but turn your jeans upside down to make it easier to pull the comma strokes.

3 Pick up a little Licorice on the Inca Gold-loaded brush and paint the large leaf, keeping the black to the outer edge to create dimension. Fill in the middle with Inca Gold.

4 With Metallic Pure Gold Dimensional paint, outline the leaf with a wavy line, then pull a little curl at the leaf tip.

5 Begin the "lace" effect on the leaf with filigree lines of Metallic Pure Gold Dimensional.

6 Fill in the rest of the leaf with the filigree. Don't overdo, let the background color show through the "lace."

7 With Licorice on a no. 8 flat, paint a couple of clusters of small one-stroke leaves and stems.

10 Add a curl of Swarovski crystals in Citrine color using the 4mm metal tip on the electric applicator (see page 21 for step-by-step instructions). Be sure the paint is dry before adding the crystals so you don't smear it.

8 Add curlicues with Licorice dimensional, and outline only one side of each black one-stroke leaf (not both sides). Outline the lacy leaf and pull a center vein.

9 Outline some of the comma strokes and scrolls with Glitter Gold dimensional and add more curlicues and tendrils if you wish. If you don't like glitter on your jeans, you can skip this step.

linen swing jacket

MATERIALS NEEDED

Colors: Thicket, Yellow Citron, Pure Orange, Yellow Light, Light Red Oxide, Magenta, Wicker White, Yellow Ochre, Lemon Custard Dimensional, Fresh Foliage Dimensional

Brushes: nos. 8 and 12 flats, 3/4-inch (19mm) flat, 1/2-inch (13mm) scruffy

Surface: Linen blend swing jacket, sage green, from Coldwater Creek. Similar jackets are available at department or specialty stores. Wash and dry jacket following label directions before painting to remove sizing. Do not use liquid fabric softener or fabric softener sheets in the dryer—this will prevent good adhesion of the paint.

Additional Supplies: Swarovski Hot-Fix rhinestones in Olivine color; electric applicator with 4mm tip.

2 Double load a 3/4-inch (19mm) flat with Pure Orange and Yellow Light and basecoat the lily petals, keeping the yellow to the outside edges. Create a folded edge on one of the petals for more interest.

3 Using the chisel edge of a no. 12 flat and Light Red Oxide, shade the bases of the petals. Pull streaks of this color outward from the throat to detail the petals.

1 Place the shirt form inside the jacket to keep everything neat and smooth. Lightly pencil in the main outlines of the design on the front of the jacket on the right side. Double load a 3/4-inch (19mm) flat with Thicket and Yellow Citron and paint the stems and leaves, keeping the Yellow Citron to the outside edge.

4 Double load a no. 12 flat with Magenta and Yellow Light and paint the sideview daisy above the orange lily using a serrated-tip petal stroke (see page 19 for instructions).

5 Pounce on the center with Thicket and Yellow Citron double loaded on a 1/2-inch (13mm) scruffy.

6 The large, pink, open daisy petals are painted with Magenta and Yellow Light double loaded on a no. 12 flat. Pick up Wicker White on the yellow side to paint the back petals that overlap the orange lily. Pounce on the daisy center with Thicket and Yellow Citron double loaded on a 1/2-inch (13mm) scruffy.

7 Double load a no. 8 flat with two-thirds Yellow Ochre and one-third Yellow Light. Add Wicker White to the Yellow Light side. Paint the two little five-petal flowers below the large pink daisy. Dot on Yellow Light centers with the tip end of the brush handle.

8 With Lemon Custard dimensional, outline the petals of the orange lily and the pink daisy and add detail lines radiating from the center.

9 With Fresh Foliage dimensional, dot the base of the sideview daisy; draw stamens coming out from the throat of the orange lily; then dot the shaded side of the large daisy center. Come back in with Lemon Custard dimensional and add the yellow pollen tips to the lily anthers.

10 If you wish, add a few Swarovski crystals in Olivine color to the centers of the pink daisies using the 4mm metal tip on the electric applicator (see page 21 for instructions). Let the paint dry thoroughly before adding the crystals.

watercolor tee

MATERIALS NEEDED

Colors: Coastal Blue, Metallic Blue Topaz, Thicket, Yellow Citron, Rose Shimmer Metallic, Wicker White, Metallic Peridot Dimensional, Lemon Custard Dimensional, Yellow Light.

Brushes: no. 12 flat, 5/8-inch (16mm) angular, no. 2 script liner.

Surface: Plain white, scoop-neck ladies' tee shirt, available at any department or specialty store. Machine wash and dry before painting to remove sizing. Do not use liquid fabric softener or fabric softener sheets in the dryer—this will prevent good adhesion of the paint.

Additional Supplies: Two small spray bottles of clean water; fabric painting shirt form.

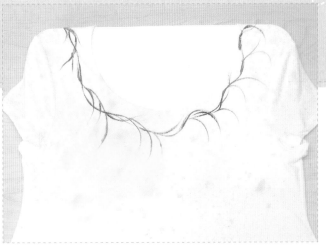

1 For the pale blue watercolor background around the neckline, squeeze about a tablespoon of Coastal Blue and a tablespoon of Metallic Blue Topaz into a small spray bottle of clean water and swish it around until blended a bit. Have a second spray bottle of clean water ready. Practice spraying the watery blue mix on a scrap piece of white cloth first to see the splatter effect you will get. Place the painting form in the tee-shirt to smooth out the fabric. Spritz the color on lightly wherever you want it. Immediately take the second bottle of clean water and spray over the blue to soften the splatters and give the look of a watercolor background. Let dry before going on.

2 With a damp paper towel, wipe off the shirt form to remove the overspray from step 1, wipe dry and re-insert it into the tee. Smooth out the neckline area. Double load a 5/8-inch (16mm) angular brush with Thicket and Yellow Citron and paint the main vines and stems around the scoop neckline.

3 Double load a no. 12 flat with the same two greens and paint long slender leaves coming off the vine. Lift to the chisel edge to create the pointed tip of the leaf.

4 Paint more long slender leaves to fill in around the neckline.

5 Double load Rose Shimmer Metallic and Wicker White on a no. 12 flat. Paint the first layer of the fuchsia blossom, keeping the white to the outside and wiggling your brush to make the ruffled edge.

6 Add more wiggle-edge petals for the outer layer. Be sure they all start and end at the stem.

7 The dark pink petals that stand up are Metallic Rose Shimmer. Paint these like long, slender leaves with pointed tips using a no. 12 flat.

8 Draw in the green stamens with Metallic Peridot dimensional, and dot on pollen with Lemon Custard dimensional.

9 Double load a no. 12 flat with Yellow Light and Wicker White and paint the butterfly's back wings. Use "serrated-tip petal" strokes and pull from the base where the wings will attach to the body.

10 The front wings are painted with the same colors but let the white edge of the brush define and separate the wings. The body and antennae are painted with Thicket and Yellow Citron on a no. 2 script liner.

11 Fill in your design with more fuchsia blossoms, varying their sizes and scattering them among the leaves. Let all the paint dry completely before wearing your tee.

MATERIALS NEEDED

Colors: Thicket, Metallic Peridot, Engine Red, Lemon Custard, Wicker White.

Brushes: nos. 12 and 16 flats, no. 6 filbert.

Surface: Dressy black twill pants from The Gap. Similar pants are available at department or specialty stores. Wash and dry following label directions before painting to remove sizing. Do not use liquid fabric softener or fabric softener sheets in the dryer—this will prevent good adhesion of the paint.

2 Double load Engine Red and Lemon Custard on a no. 12 flat and begin the petals of the main flower. Each petal is a touch and pull stroke starting at the outer tip and pulling in toward the stem.

3 Working upward from the bottom of the petal cluster, fill in more petals. Turn your surface to make pulling the strokes easier.

1 This design is inspired by old tapestries with their stylized flowers and leaves. Double load Thicket and Metallic Peridot on a no. 16 flat and chisel edge the main vines and stems for placement on the front of the pants leg.

4 Paint the two side pods with two side-by-side strokes. Start at the outside tip, press down and stroke upward, lifting to the chisel edge of the brush. If you're painting on black, you may need to overstroke to get good coverage.

5 Paint three little comma strokes coming out of the ends of the pods—pick up more Lemon Custard on your brush so they're a little more yellow than the flower petals.

6 Add two more flower clusters above the first one using the same colors and brush.

6

7 Stroke green sepals over some of the pink petals using Metallic Peridot and a touch of Lemon Custard.

8 Double load a no. 16 flat with Wicker White and Engine Red plus a little Lemon Custard, and base in the curved shapes of the two lower halves of the large flower pods.

9 Form the ruffly edge of the back part of the pod, keeping the yellow side of the brush to the top.

10 Re-load with the same colors and form the ruffly edge of the front of the pod the same way, keeping the yellow side of the brush to the top to clearly indicate the front edge.

11 Finish the pod on the other side of the stem using the same brush and colors.

12 Paint the upper cup-shapes of the flower pods the same way using the no. 16 flat and Wicker White, Engine Red and a little Lemon Custard. Turn your surface as needed to make pulling the strokes easier.

14 The front half of the curled leaf is painted with a little more Lemon Custard on the brush. Paint the leaf in distinct segments.

13 Begin the large curled leaf below the flower cluster using the same dirty brush sideloaded into Metallic Peridot and a little Lemon Custard. Paint the back half of the leaf first, keeping the Peridot to the outside ruffled edge of the leaf.

15 Double load a no. 12 flat with Metallic Peridot and Lemon Custard, alternating with Wicker White. Paint the center vein of the leaf, then begin to add small leaves to form the curled outer tip.

16 Add progressively larger leaf segments as you go up the center vein. Keep the lighter side of your brush to the outside so that each segment is clearly outlined and separate.

17 Highlight the center of the leaf with a double load of Metallic Peridot and Lemon Custard; paint a series of comma strokes to indicate leaf segments.

18 With the same colors you've been using all along, add a few extra stems and leaves here and there to elongate and fill in the design above and below the large segmented leaf you just painted. The larger leaves have ruffled edges and the smaller red ones are one-stroke leaves.

19 Double load a no. 6 filbert with Engine Red and Lemon Custard, and sprinkle some tiny one-stroke leaves at the ends of the stems above the main flower cluster and wherever the design looks a little empty. With Metallic Peridot dimensional, draw some tendrils and curls among the flowers and outline the large flower pods.

20 Finish with more tendrils, curls and swirls of Metallic Peridot dimensional paint above and below the large segmented leaf. Outline and detail the ruffled leaves as much or as little as you want.

classic denim jacket

MATERIALS NEEDED

Colors: Engine Red, Yellow Light, Thicket, Yellow Citron, Licorice Dimensional.

Brush: no. 16 flat.

Surface: Classic denim jacket, hip length, from Coldwater Creek. Similar jackets available at any department or specialty store. Machine wash and dry before painting to remove sizing. Do not use liquid fabric softener or fabric softener sheets in the dryer—this will prevent good adhesion of the paint.

1 Begin on the back of the jacket. Load one flat side of a no. 16 flat in Engine Red and load the other flat side in Yellow Light. Stroke the upper back cupped petals with the red side first, then flip the brush over and stroke with the yellow side. Don't overblend.

2 Stroke a series of shorter front petals the same way.

3 The two drooping petals are stroked in as two large commas. If the yellow isn't showing up, pick up more on your brush each time you stroke. Add a smaller blossom to the right.

4 Double load Thicket and Yellow Citron and chisel edge the stems. Paint long slender leaves coming up from the base of the stem. If your brush still has a little red and yellow in it from the tulip petals, that's fine.

5 Using Licorice dimensional, loosely outline and detail the tulips to separate the petals. Outline the leaves and stems too. Add curls and loops.

6 If you want to repeat this design on the front of the jacket, vary it a little by adding leaves and stems only to the small tulip. On the collar and pockets, add lacy filigree lines using Licorice dimensional (see page 15 for instructions).

tailored shirt

MATERIALS NEEDED

Colors: Wicker White, Pearl White Dimensional.

Brushes: nos. 8 and 12 flats.

Surface: Pink cotton tailored shirt, available at department or specialty stores. Wash and dry following label directions before painting to remove sizing. Do not use liquid fabric softener or fabric softener sheets in the dryer—this will prevent good adhesion of the paint.

Additional Supplies: Fabric painting shirt form; small clamps.

1 Place the shirt form inside and clamp at both sides to keep the fabric smooth. Using Pearl White dimensional paint on a no. 12 flat, draw the curving lines that delineate the bottom edge of the design on both sides of the shirt front.

2 Dress a no. 12 flat with fabric medium and sideload in Wicker White. Paint an overlapping series of five-petal flowers clustered tightly together in the areas above the bottom edge.

3 Fill in all the way up to the shoulder seam and under the collar. Fold the collar inward to make it easier to paint in this area.

4 Load a no. 8 flat with Wicker White and paint little one stroke leaves to fill in among the flowers.

5 Applying Pearl White dimensional with the tip of the bottle, outline the flowers and the largest leaves. Also create a lacy edge along the bottom line by making freehand loops and squiggles, then dot along the line above the loops to look like little French knots.

6 Repeat this entire design on the other side of the shirt front. Hang to let the paint dry completely before wearing.

long a-line skirt

MATERIALS NEEDED

Colors: Metallic Rose Shimmer, Engine Red, Yellow Light, Yellow Ochre, Thicket, Yellow Citron, Wicker White, Fresh Foliage Dimensional.

Brushes: no. 8 flat, 3/4-inch (19mm) flat, 1/2-inch (13mm) scruffy.

Surface: White, A-line, linen-blend skirt, calf-length, available at any department or specialty store during spring and summer. Machine wash and dry before painting to remove sizing. Do not use liquid fabric softener or fabric softener sheets in the dryer—this will prevent good adhesion of the paint.

Additional Supplies: Swarovski Hot-Fix rhinestones in Citrine color; electric applicator with 4mm metal tip.

1 Double load Metallic Rose Shimmer and Yellow Light on a 3/4-inch (19mm) flat and begin painting large flower petals with ruffly outer edges.

2 Complete the large pink flower with a total of six petals. Pounce in the center using Yellow Ochre on a 1/2-inch (13mm) scruffy.

3 Double load a no. 8 flat with Rose Shimmer Metallic and Engine Red. Stay up on the chisel edge and pull fine vein lines out from the center on each petal. Outline the outside edge of each petal and the center with Fresh Foliage dimensional.

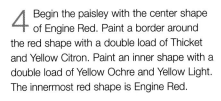

4 Begin the paisley with the center shape of Engine Red. Paint a border around the red shape with a double load of Thicket and Yellow Citron. Paint an inner shape with a double load of Yellow Ochre and Yellow Light. The innermost red shape is Engine Red.

5 Place stems and leaves using a double load of Thicket and Yellow Citron. Dot Wicker White dimensional around the yellow part of the paisley.

6 Double load a 3/4-inch (19mm) flat with Thicket and Yellow Citron and paint the largest leaf coming out from beneath the large flower. Add a few smaller leaves and stems below the large leaf.

7 If you wish, add pre-glued Swarovski crystals in the Citrine color to the centers of the large flowers using the heated applicator (see page 21 for instructions). Be sure the paint in this area is dry before applying them. Finish by detailing and outlining the leaves and paisleys and adding curlicues and tendrils with Fresh Foliage dimensional.

sparkly camisole

MATERIALS NEEDED

Colors: Autumn Leaves, Light Red Oxide, Vintage Orange, Wicker White.

Brushes: no. 16 flat, 1/2-inch (13mm) scruffy, large scruffy.

Surface: White cotton-spandex camisole, available at department or specialty stores. Wash and dry following label directions before painting to remove sizing. Do not use liquid fabric softener or fabric softener sheets in the dryer—this will prevent good adhesion of the paint.

Additional Supplies: Fabric painting shirt form; fabric medium; Ultrafine Art Glitter in Nugget, Melone, and Mustard colors; clear glitter adhesive (optional), Swarovski Hot-Fix rhinestones in Volcano and Clear Diamond colors; electric applicator with 4mm metal tip.

1 Place the shirt form inside the camisole to smooth out the fabric. Clamp the straps behind so they don't get paint on them. Double load a 1/2-inch (13mm) scruffy with Autumn Leaves and Light Red Oxide. Pounce in the center of the sunflower. The neckline of this camisole is straight, so only half of the center is included in the design.

2 Double load a no. 16 flat with Vintage Orange and Wicker White and pick up a little Fabric Medium. Begin painting the large pointed sunflower petals, starting at the brown center, pressing down to widen the petal, and lifting to the chisel to form the pointed tip.

3 For the darker petals, pull some of the brown from the center as you stroke the petal outward.

4 For the next layer of lighter petals, use the same dirty brush and pick up mostly Wicker White on your brush. These petals are shorter and placed between the first layer's petals. For more interest, pick up a little bit of Autumn Leaves and stroke a few really short petals.

5 Re-establish and clean up the edge of the flower center with the scruffy and Autumn Leaves and Light Red Oxide. If you want to add Art Glitter to the center, do so while the paint is still wet; the glitter will stick only to the wet areas. Or let the paint dry, apply clear glitter adhesive, then spoon on the glitter. Here, I'm using Nugget for the darkest color, Melone for the orange outer ring and Mustard for the very center. When all the paint dries, brush off any excess glitter with a large scruffy.

6 Apply crystals to the glitter area if you wish. These are Swarovski Hot-Fix rhinestones in Volcano and Clear Diamond colors.

satin ballet flats

MATERIALS NEEDED

Colors: Licorice, Metallic Inca Gold, Metallic Silver Sterling, Metallic Silver Dimensional.

Brush: no. 6 flat.

Surface: Black satin ballet flats from Target. Similar flats are available at department or specialty stores.

Additional Supplies: Fabric Medium; Swarovski Hot-Fix rhinestones in Clear Diamond; electric applicator with 4mm metal tip.

1 Load a no. 6 flat in Licorice and sideload into Metallic Inca Gold. Begin painting the gold six-petal flowers on the toe of the shoe. It's easier and faster to paint both shoes at the same time and your colors will be more consistent.

2 Add more gold flowers and little one-stroke leaves, but leave plenty of room for the silver flowers and other flourishes to come.

3 Begin painting the silver six-petal flowers by loading the no. 6 flat into Licorice, then sideloading into Metallic Silver Sterling. Don't forget to pick up some fabric medium on your loaded brush if it begins to drag.

4 Fill in with more silver flowers and little one-stroke leaves. Depending on the style of your ballet flats, you may be able to continue the design along the sides of the shoes. Use the Metallic Silver dimensional to draw stems and tendrils and to outline the silver flowers.

5 If you wish, attach clear crystals to a few (not all) of the flower centers, using Swarovski Hot-Fix rhinestones in Clear Diamond and an electric applicator with a 4mm metal tip that heats the glue on the back of each crystal (see page 21 for complete instructions).

6 Let the paint dry completely before wearing the shoes. Store them in a protective shoe box to keep the paint from being scraped or nicked.

butterfly socks

MATERIALS NEEDED

Colors: Metallic Amethyst, Wicker White, Thicket, Yellow Citron, Yellow Light, Brilliant Blue, Coastal Blue.

Brushes: no. 12 flat, no. 2 script liner.

Surface: Girls' socks in coral pink, white and light green from Target. Similar socks are available at department or specialty stores. Machine wash and dry before painting to remove sizing. Do not use liquid fabric softener or fabric softener sheets in the dryer—this will prevent good adhesion of the paint.

Additional Supplies: Fabric Medium.

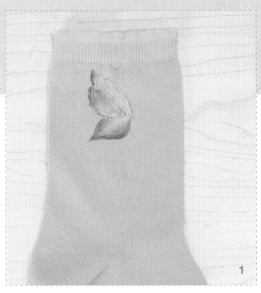

1 Paint your design on the upper part of the cuff on the outer side. Double load a no. 12 flat with Metallic Amethyst and Wicker White and paint the back wings of the butterfly, keeping the purple to the outside edges of the wings.

2 Re-load with the same colors, picking up more Wicker White this time, and paint the front wings, keeping the white to the outside edges of the wings.

3 Paint the butterfly body segments, head and antennae with Thicket and Yellow Citron double loaded on a no. 2 script liner.

4 Detail the wings with spots and comma strokes using Yellow Light and Wicker White on a no. 12 flat.

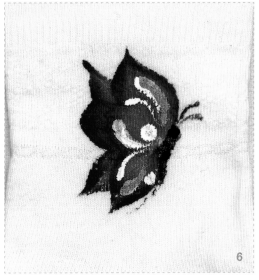

5 The colors for the butterfly on the green socks are:
Wings: Yellow Light and Wicker White.
Body, Head & Antennae: Thicket & Yellow Citron.
Details on Wings: Wicker White, Brilliant Blue and Coastal Blue.

6 The colors for the butterfly on the white socks are:
Wings: Brilliant Blue and Coastal Blue.
Body, Head & Antennae: Thicket and Yellow Citron.
Details on Wings: Yellow Citron and Wicker White.

dressy clutch purse

MATERIALS NEEDED

Colors: Metallic Taupe, Metallic Silver Sterling, Licorice, Glitter Silver Dimensional.

Brush: no. 6 flat.

Surface: Black satin evening clutch from J.C. Penney. Similar purses are available at department or specialty stores.

Additional Supplies: Fabric Medium; Swarovski Hot-Fix rhinestones in Clear Diamond; electric applicator with 4mm metal tip.

1 Double load a no. 6 flat with Metallic Taupe and Metallic Silver Sterling and paint a couple of clusters of comma strokes to begin the flowers.

2 Fill in with more Metallic Taupe comma strokes. Paint a smaller cluster of comma strokes to the left of the larger blossom.

3 Chisel edge the stems with Metallic Taupe. Load the no. 6 flat with Licorice, sideload into Metallic Taupe and paint the scalloped-edge leaf.

4 Add dry-brushed comma strokes with Metallic Taupe and little one-stroke leaves with Metallic Silver Sterling.

5 With Glitter Silver dimensional, go over the stems, and add some long curls and scrolls extending out to the side. This paint looks white when it comes out but in 15 minutes will dry to a glittery silver. Let it dry overnight before touching the paint.

6 Apply crystals to the glitter area if you wish. These are Swarovski Hot-Fix rhinestones in Clear Diamond. Use the electric applicator with the 4mm metal tip (see page 21 for complete instructions).

casual handbag

MATERIALS NEEDED

Colors: Hauser Green Medium, Yellow Citron, Brilliant Blue, Wicker White, Engine Red, Yellow Light, Lemon Custard Dimensional, Fresh Foliage Dimensional.

Brushes: nos 10 and 12 flats, no. 10 filbert.

Surface: Sage green nylon handbag from Target. Similar handbags are available at department or specialty stores.

Additional Supplies: Fabric Medium.

1 Double load a no. 12 flat with Hauser Green Medium and Yellow Citron and place in the main vines and stems. Depending on the color of your purse, you may need to choose other greens.

2 With the same colors, paint long slender leaves. You may need to stroke them twice to get good coverage.

3 For the morning glories, double load a no. 12 flat with Brilliant Blue and Wicker White. Paint the base of the large, open flower in the center, and the back petals and the base of the sideview flower on the right.

4 Pick up more Wicker White on the dirty brush and paint the front petals of the sideview flower on the right. Wiggle the brush for the upper edge of the petal, then pull down to the base.

5 Paint the back of the open trumpet of the center flower the same way—wiggle the brush to form the scalloped edge at the top, then pull down to the base.

6 Fill in the front of the trumpet the same way. Shade the throat by picking up more Brilliant Blue on the brush and doing a series of wiggle strokes around the center.

7 The twisted bud at the left is painted with five overlapping comma strokes using a double load of Brilliant Blue and Wicker White.

8 With a no. 10 filbert, paint the red five-petal flowers using Engine Red. Add a few trailing buds here and there. Pick up Brilliant Blue on the dirty brush and shade the red petals.

9 Double load Yellow Light and Wicker White on a no. 10 flat and add the yellow flowers using the chisel edge of the brush and very short strokes. These flowers are wider at the base and narrower at the tip.

10 Using Lemon Custard dimensional, dot in the flower centers on the open morning glory and the red five-petal flowers. Texture the yellow flowers by drawing short curving lines with a "squeeze-release" motion on the bottle.

11 Outline and detail the leaves with Fresh Foliage dimensional and add tendrils and curlicues if you like. Let the paint dry completely before using your purse.

elegant evening wrap

MATERIALS NEEDED

Colors: Metallic Taupe, Metallic Peridot, Inca Gold Metallic, Licorice Dimensional.

Brushes: no. 12 flat, no. 8 filbert.

Surface: Black acrylic fringed shawl from Target. Similar shawls are available at department or specialty stores.

Additional Supplies: Fabric Medium; Ultrafine Opaque Art Glitter in "Nugget" color; Swarovski Hot-Fix rhinestones in AB Volcano color; electric applicator with 4mm metal tip.

1 Load a no. 12 flat with Metallic Taupe and paint graceful curves of large and small comma strokes across the bottom edge of the shawl.

2 With Metallic Peridot on a no. 12 flat, paint large single-stroke leaves here and there among the comma strokes.

3 Load a no. 8 filbert with Inca Gold Metallic and paint the little five-petal flowers. Paint some of them open, some side view, and some trailing petals.

4 With Licorice Dimensional, paint some long curls and tendrils that echo the shapes of the comma strokes.

5 While the black curls and tendrils are still wet, spoon Ultrafine Art Glitter in "Nugget" color over them. Let the shawl sit undisturbed until all the paint is completely dry, then brush off excess glitter with a large scruffy.

6 Apply Swarovski Hot-Fix rhinestones in "AB Volcano" color to the centers of the gold flowers. Use the electric applicator with the 4mm metal tip (see page 21 for complete instructions).

laptop computer bag

MATERIALS NEEDED

Colors: Yellow Citron, Thicket, Berry Wine, Engine Red, Yellow Light, Wicker White, Pure Orange, Metallic Peridot Dimensional, Metallic Pure Gold Dimensional, Engine Red Dimensional.

Brushes: nos. 12 and 16 flats, no. 2 script liner, 1/2-inch (13mm) scruffy.

Surface: Black microfiber carry-on bag from Target. Similar computer bags are available at department or specialty stores. Look for ones with a large smooth area for painting.

Additional Supplies: Fabric Medium.

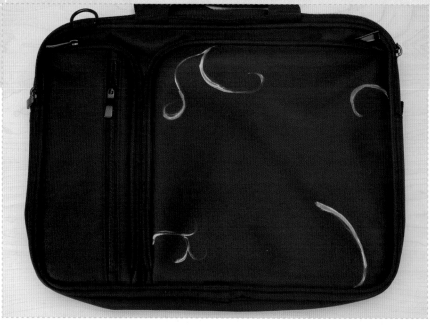

2 Multi-load a no. 16 flat with Berry Wine and Engine Red on one side of the brush and Yellow Light and Wicker White on the other side. Stroke on wiggle edge leaves starting with the center leaf, then overlap the two outer leaves, keeping the yellow side of the brush to the outside edges of the leaves.

1 Load a no. 2 script liner with Yellow Citron, pick up a little Thicket and place in the main stems. You may need to overstroke a few times for best coverage.

3 Pick up Pure Orange on the red side of the dirty brush and begin painting the outer skirt of petals of the blossom.

4 Finish the outer skirt of the petals, then pick up more Engine Red and stroke teardrop shapes for the inner skirt of petals.

5 Double load Thicket and Yellow Citron on a no. 12 flat. Paint one-stroke leaves and comma strokes around and in the flower.

6 With the same brush and colors, paint long comma strokes coming off the stem of the flower.

7 Double load a 1/2-inch (13mm) scruffy with Yellow Light and Wicker White and pounce on the flower center.

9 Double load a no. 16 flat with Thicket and Yellow Citron, pick up a little Engine Red on the light green side. Paint one side of the ruffled-edge leaf with a slide out-wiggle-slide back stroke.

10 Paint the other half the same way, keeping the lighter side of your brush to the outside edge of the leaf.

8 Draw a series of short curved lines for the stamens in the flower center with Metallic Peridot dimensional. Outline and detail the leaves and stems with Metallic Peridot dimensional. Outline the flower blossom with Metallic Pure Gold dimensional.

11 Fill in the design with a variety of leaves. Paint a large, cupped acanthus leaf using the same greens and red on a no. 16 flat.

12 If your bag has an extra pocket on the front, you can paint a coordinating design of repeating leaves using the same colors. Begin with Yellow Citron stems and fill in with small one-stroke leaves in the same reds and greens used for the main part of the design. Outline and detail many of the leaves with Engine Red dimensional.

13 Finish by outlining and detailing all the leaves and adding curls and tendrils using the dimensional paints in Metallic Peridot, Metallic Pure Gold, and Engine Red.

wedding album

MATERIALS NEEDED

Colors: Yellow Ochre, Wicker White.

Brush: no. 12 flat.

Surface: Ivory fabric-covered photo album and light green fabric-covered photo album, both from Target. Similar photo albums are available at department or specialty stores.

Additional Supplies: Fabric Medium.

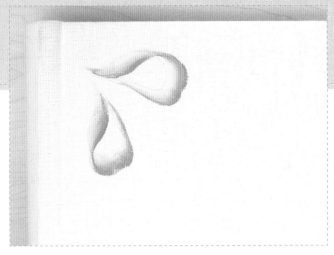

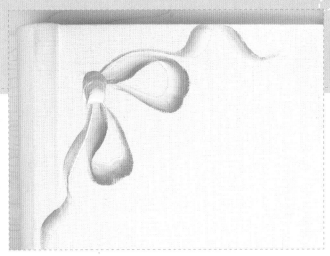

1 Double load Yellow Ochre and Wicker White on a no. 12 flat and paint the large open loops of the ribbon. These two colors are used throughout.

2 Continue the tails of the ribbon down the side and along the top, letting it disappear off the edge then reappear again. The center knot is made up of two C-strokes.

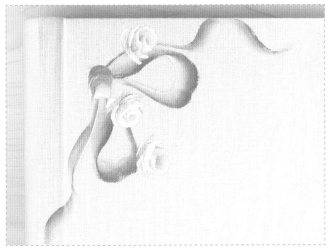

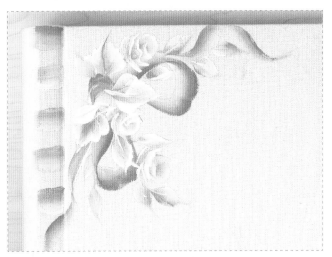

3 Pick up lots more Wicker White on the white side of the no. 12 flat and paint three opening rose buds, keeping the white to the outer edges of the petals.

4 Add little one-stroke leaves among the rose buds, and finish with short horizontal stripes along the spine of the album.

Use the same paint colors and design elements to create a lovely decorative frame around the photo opening on this light green fabric-covered memory album. Switch to a no. 8 flat and double load with Yellow Ochre and Wicker White. Paint little roses at each corner, then fill in with one-strokes leaves.

floral photo album

MATERIALS NEEDED

Colors: Metallic Peridot, Thicket, Wicker White, Yellow Ochre, Metallic Amethyst, Glitter Ice Sparkle Dimensional.

Brushes: 5/8-inch (16mm) angular, no. 12 flat.

Surface: Black fabric-covered photo album from Target. Similar photo albums are available at department or specialty stores.

Additional Supplies: Fabric Medium.

1 Double load Metallic Peridot and Thicket on a 5/8-inch (16mm) angular brush with Thicket on the toe (longer side) of the bristles. Lead with the heel (shorter side) and paint the large background leaves. To vary the leaf color, pick up Wicker White sometimes. Use the chisel edge to pull stems into the leaves. Paint comma strokes with long curving tails.

2 Double load the 5/8-inch (16mm) angular brush with two-thirds Yellow Ochre and one-third Wicker White on the toe of the brush. Begin painting the large cabbage rose with the outer skirt of petals, picking up fresh Wicker White on the toe for each stroke. I've already painted the smaller rose underneath so you can see where you're headed.

3 Paint the second layer of the outer skirt of the rose the same way, but make these strokes shorter so the first layer can still be seen.

4 Double load the 5/8-inch (16mm) angular brush with Yellow Ochre on the heel and Wicker White on the toe. Paint the back petal of the center bowl of the rose. Paint the front of the bowl, then pull two smaller side petals across the front of the bowl, one from the left and one from the right. Keep the Wicker White side of the brush always to the outer edges of the petals as you stroke.

5 Continue pulling in more petals from both sides across the front of the bowl to finish the cabbage rose. Turn your surface as needed to making pulling these strokes easier.

6 Fill in the design with smaller roses that are just opening from bud stage, using the same brush and colors.

8 Paint the drooping leaves under the opening rose buds with Metallic Peridot and Wicker White double loaded on the 5/8-inch (16mm) angular brush.

7 For the lavender leaves, switch to a no. 12 flat and load with Metallic Amethyst. Pick up a little Wicker White on the brush and paint one stroke leaves. Pull chisel edge stems into them.

9 With Glitter Ice Sparkle dimensional, draw a series of curls over some of the large leaves and extending outward from the design. As the Glitter paint dries, the glue will turn clear and the glitter will be turquoise blue.

christening gown

MATERIALS NEEDED

Colors: Metallic Peridot, Wicker White, Lavender, Lemon Custard.

Brushes: nos. 6 and 8 flats, no. 2 script liner.

Surface: White cotton christening gown with lace trim, from Wimpole Street Creations, 501 W. 900 North, N. Salt Lake City, Utah 84054, phone (801) 298-0504. Wash the gown to remove sizing and let hang to dry before painting. Iron if needed. Do not use fabric softener in the rinse water; this will prevent good adhesion of the paint.

Additional Supplies: Fabric Medium.

1 Double load Metallic Peridot and Wicker White on a no. 8 flat and paint the large leaves and the small one-stroke leaves. If your brush begins to drag, dip into fabric medium when you reload your colors. Pull chisel-edge stems partway into the centers of the larger leaves.

2 Load a no. 6 flat in Wicker White and pick up a little Lavender and begin painting the lighter violets, keeping the Lavender side to the outside edges of the petals. Each violet is a little five-petal flower.

3 Fill in as much as you want with more violets, picking up more Lavender on your brush for the darker ones.

4 When you have filled in as many violets as you want in the cluster, dot in yellow centers on the open violets with Lemon Custard using a no. 2 script liner. Allow a few single petals and some tiny leaves to trail away from the bottom of the main cluster to give the design an airy and delicate look.

5 Repeat the design on the gown wherever needed, adapting the shape and size depending on the style of your gown. Here I thinned the colors used on the main cluster and painted side clusters, making them smaller, shorter and much less dense.

ringbearer's pillow

MATERIALS NEEDED

Colors: Metallic Inca Gold, Wicker White, Metallic Taupe, Pearl Champagne Dimensional.

Brush: no. 2 script liner.

Surface: White satin heart-shaped ringbearer's pillow, from Jo-Ann's Fabric stores.

Additional Supplies: Fabric Medium.

1 Double load a no. 2 script liner with Inca Gold Metallic and Wicker White. Begin this simple strokework design with comma stroke scrolls at the bottom of the heart-shaped pillow.

2 Build the scroll design depending on the size and shape of the pillow. Work around the ribbon in the upper center that will tie the rings to the pillow.

3 Add richness to the colors by adding scrolls of Metallic Taupe, which gives a silvery look to the pillow in case the wedding rings are white gold or platinum.

4 Finish with tiny curls of Pearl Champagne dimensional to fill in empty areas and to detail some of the scrollwork with dots of paint. These will look like tiny seed pearls when dry. Be sure to allow plenty of time for all the paint to dry completely before tying the rings to the pillow with the ribbon.

baby bibs

MATERIALS NEEDED

Colors: Lavender, Wicker White, Orchid, Lemon Custard, Metallic Peridot, Metallic Blue Topaz, Yellow Citron.

Brushes: nos. 6, 8 and 12 flats, no. 2 script liner.

Surface: White cotton baby bibs, from Wimpole Street Creations, 501 W. 900 North, N. Salt Lake City, Utah 84054, phone (801) 298-0504. Wash and dry the bibs to remove sizing before painting. Do not use fabric softener in the rinse water or fabric softener sheets in the dryer; this will prevent good adhesion of the paint.

Additional Supplies: Fabric Medium.

1 Double load Lavender and Wicker White on a no. 12 flat and paint three curving, nested strokes to form the upper part of one wing.

2 Paint a single stroke for the bottom part of the wing. Keep the white side of the brush to the upper edge of the wing and lift to the chisel edge as you pull the stroke to a point.

3 Re-load your no. 12 flat with Lavender and Wicker White and paint the wings on the other side, starting with the upper one, then the lower one. Flip your brush so the Lavender forms the outside edge of the upper wing and the lower edge of the lower wing.

4 Paint the smaller pink butterfly wings the same way using a double load of Orchid and Wicker White. The smallest yellow butterfly's wings are painted with Lemon Custard and Wicker White on a no. 8 flat.

5 The segmented bodies of all three butterflies are painted with Metallic Peridot on a no. 6 flat, and the antennae are done with the no. 2 script liner. Pull a fine line, then press down on the bristles slightly to form the tip end of each antenna. This lacy bib with its pretty pastel butterflies would be a lovely gift for a baby girl.

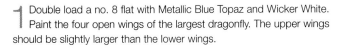

1 Double load a no. 8 flat with Metallic Blue Topaz and Wicker White. Paint the four open wings of the largest dragonfly. The upper wings should be slightly larger than the lower wings.

2 Use the same colors to paint the wings for the sideview dragonfly and the smallest dragonfly. Don't forget to pick up some fabric medium on your loaded brush if your strokes begin to drag on the material.

3 Paint the bodies and antennae with Yellow Citron on a no. 2 script liner. The bodies of the two sideview dragonflies should curve upward at the tail end, and their antennae should curve forward.

4 With the blue colors of the dragonflies and the tailored style of the bib, this would make a great gift for a baby boy.

baby bloomers

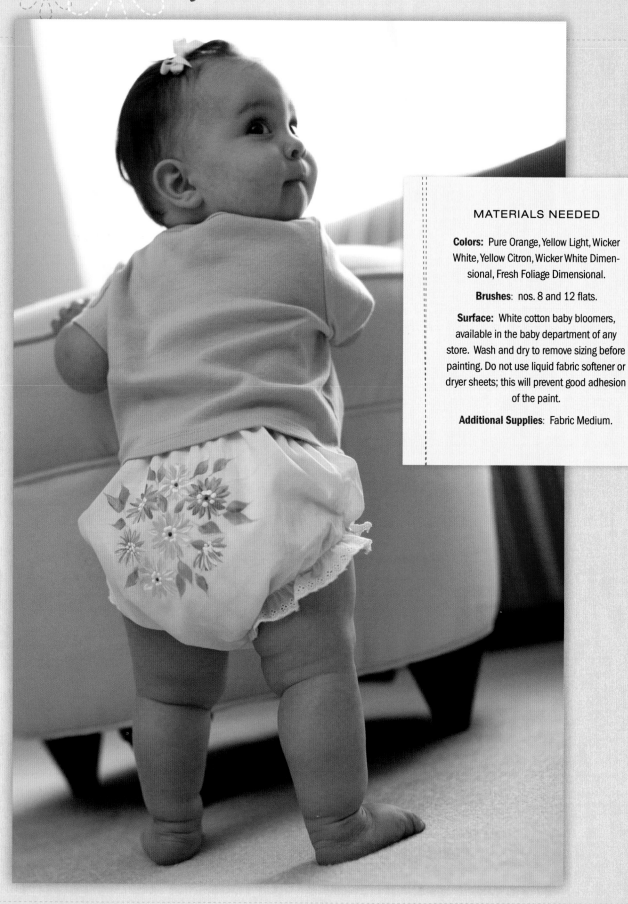

2 Fill in the orange daisy with four more petals between the four starter petals.

1 Double load Pure Orange and Yellow Light on a no. 8 flat and stroke in four daisy petals like a clockface at 3, 6, 9 and 12 noon. These are your starter petals. The yellow daisies are Yellow Light and Wicker White.

3 Fill in between those with more petals to form layers. Pick up more Pure Orange sometimes and more Yellow Light sometimes to vary the colors of the petals.

4 Add as many daisies as you want, alternating picking up more yellow, more white, or more orange to vary the flower colors. Make some of the daisies sideview and some not quite fully open. Add little one-stroke leaves around and among the daisies with Yellow Citron on a no. 12 flat. Dot in the daisy centers with a circle of Wicker White dimensional. Add a Fresh Foliage dimensional dot in dead center on some of them.

decorative pillows

MATERIALS NEEDED

Colors: Metallic Taupe, Metallic Blue Topaz, Metallic Peridot, Brilliant Blue.

Brushes: nos. 12 and 16 flats, 1/2-inch (13mm) feather brush, no. 2 script liner.

Surfaces: Sofa pillows, 14 inches (35.6cm) square, one in copper colored silk and one in light blue silk, from Linens 'N' Things. Similar silk pillows can be found at home and department stores.

Additional Supplies: Fabric Medium.

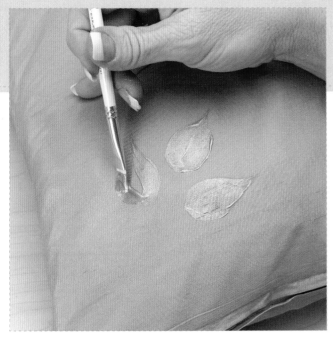

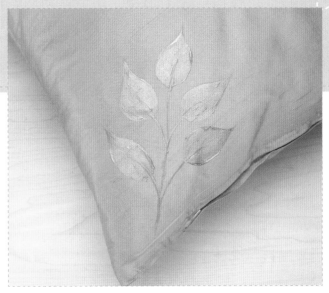

1 The copper colored silk pillow is painted with a variety of leaves and ferns using only three metallic colors to echo the sheen of the silk. Begin with the large blue leaves. Using a a no. 12 flat, make a brush mix of Metallic Taupe and Metallic Blue Topaz. Paint the leaves in two strokes, half the leaf with one stroke, the other half with another. Fill in the center. Re-load and re-stroke to get full coverage if needed.

2 Continue adding a couple more leaves to make a cluster. Pick up Metallic Peridot on the chisel edge of the dirty brush and pull stems into each one.

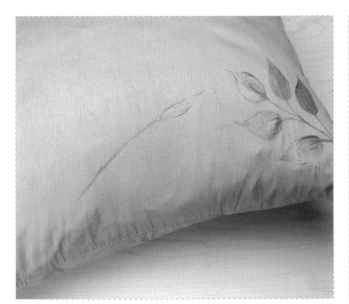

3 Begin the ferns with the center stem and the leaf at the tip, using a brush mix of Metallic Taupe and Metallic Peridot on the same dirty brush so there's a tiny bit of the blue still in the brush.

4 Fill in the fern frond with more long slender leaves coming off the main stem. These fern leaves are paired opposite each other along the stem.

5 Brush mix Metallic Taupe and Metallic Peridot and pick up a little Metallic Blue Topaz on a no. 16 flat. Paint a chisel edge stem with some stemlets coming off of it, and add a large leaf at the tip.

6 Fill in with more large leaves. For variety of shape in this cluster, wiggle one edge of each leaf and let the other side remain smooth.

7 Repeat these three leaf designs over the entire pillow, spacing them out and turning them in different directions to make a nice design. Have some of them coming up from the side and out from the corners. Keep using the same three colors on your brush and follow the directions in steps 1 through 6. Each leaf cluster should have at least two of the colors, sometimes all three, to tie the design together. Let the paint dry completely before using your pillows. Spot clean them whenever needed.

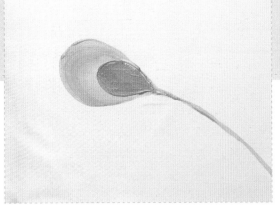

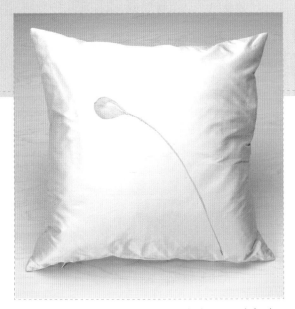

2 For the inner part of the eye, switch to a no. 12 flat and paint a teardrop shape of Metallic Blue Topaz.

1 To paint the blue silk pillow with a single peacock feather, place the spine of the feather using the chisel edge of a no. 16 flat and Metallic Peridot. Pick up Metallic Taupe on the dirty brush and paint the eye of the feather using a teardrop stroke.

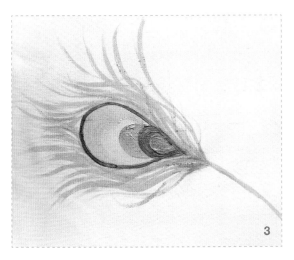

3

3 The deepest blue on the eye's center is Brilliant Blue. While it's still wet, come back in with a little Metallic Blue Topaz to add some iridescence to this spot. Outline the entire eye with only Brilliant Blue on a no. 2 script liner. Load a 1/2-inch (13mm) feather brush with Metallic Peridot and begin pulling the wispy feathers around the eye.

4 Continue working your way down the feather's spine, pulling long wispy feathers from each side using the feather brush. Add a few wispy blue feathers among the green ones to tie the colors into the eye.

5 As the wispy feathers extend from the spine's length, they get longer with more space between them. Let a few of them cross over each other and flop over a little. Don't worry if the nubby texture of the silk catches more of the paint in some places than others. When you finish with the wispy feathers, re-establish the spine with Metallic Peridot on the chisel edge of a no. 12 flat.

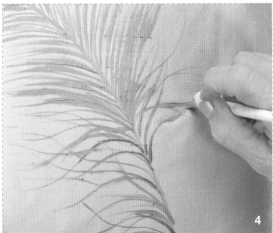

4

MATERIALS NEEDED

Colors: Metallic Peridot, Licorice, Metallic Taupe, Licorice Dimensional.

Brushes: nos. 8 and 16 flats.

Surface: Ivory waffle-weave dish towels and round pot holders in black and taupe, all from Target. Similar items are available at department or specialty stores.

Additional Supplies: Fabric Medium.

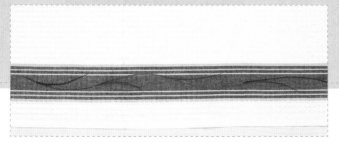 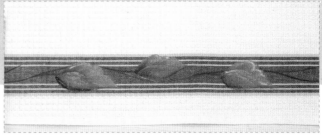

1 Look for waffle weave towels that have a decorative stripe along both long sides. This area is smoother and easier to paint on. Double load Metallic Peridot and Licorice on a no. 16 flat and chisel edge the vines along the towel's decorative stripe.

2 With the same brush and colors, paint two-stroke leaves that are wiggle-edge on one side and smooth on the other.

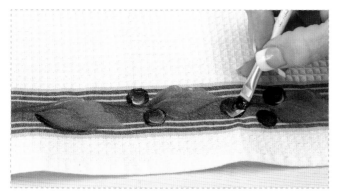 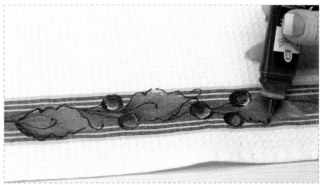

3 Load a no. 8 flat with Licorice and sideload into Metallic Taupe. Paint the berries using two half-circle strokes. Keep the Licorice side of the brush to the outside edge to shade one side of each berry.

4 Outline and detail the leaves and add the stems to the berries using Licorice dimensional.

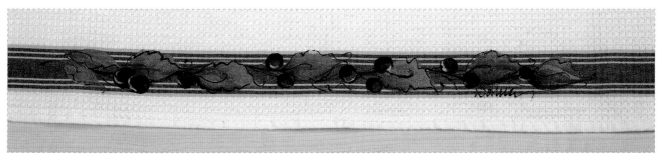

Use the same colors and design elements to paint matching pot holders. The black pot holder picks up the black used in the dish towels for a coordinated look. To paint the black pot holder, use more Metallic Taupe on your brush to paint the berries and outline the leaves and stems with Metallic Peridot. If you prefer a lighter-colored pot holder such as the taupe one, use more Licorice in your brush when you paint the berries and outline the leaves and draw stems with Licorice dimensional.

MATERIALS NEEDED

Colors: Asphaltum, Wicker White, Magenta, Lemon Custard, Thicket, Yellow Citron, Brilliant Blue, Lavender, Inca Gold Metallic, Metallic Pure Gold Dimensional.

Brushes: nos. 6, 8, 12 and 16 flats, no. 2 script liner.

Surface: Sage green cotton-blend round tablecloth from Target. Similar tablecloths are available at department or specialty stores. Wash and dry tablecloth before painting to remove sizing. Don't use liquid fabric softener or dryer sheets—this will prevent good adhesion of the paint.

Additional Supplies: Fabric Medium.

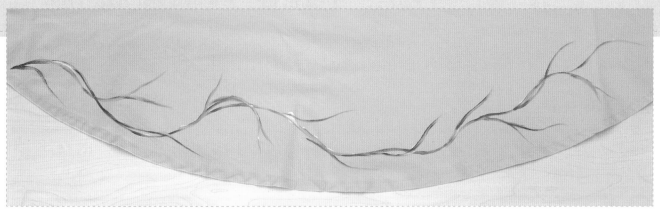

1 Double load a no. 16 flat with Asphaltum plus a little Wicker White and place the main grapevine around the border of the round tablecloth, letting it curve and change direction but following the curve of the cloth. Don't get too close to the edge—leave enough space to fill in with fruits and leaves.

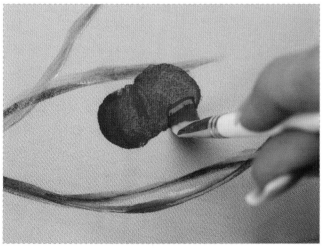

2 Double load a no. 12 flat with two-thirds Magenta and one-third Asphaltum. Begin painting the large strawberries by stroking in a pumpkin shape for the upper part. Turn your brush so the Asphaltum side is to the outside edge of the berry to shade it and give roundness.

3 Under the pumpkin shape add the bottom point of the strawberry, keeping the Asphaltum side of the brush to the outside edge to shade.

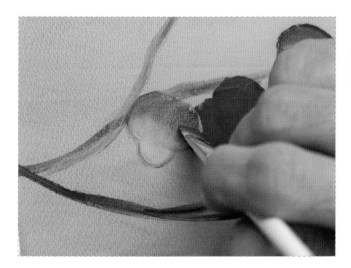

4 To paint some berries that aren't quite ripe, pick up Lemon Custard and stroke yellow across the top of the berry. For an unripe berry like this one, base in first with Lemon Custard, then come back in with Magenta on the dirty brush and add a bit of pink to the berry.

5 Load a no. 2 script liner with Asphaltum, pick up some Wicker White and stroke on tiny lines for the seeds. The seeds on the lower, shaded part of the berry should be darker than the highlighted seeds on the upper part.

6 With Thicket and Yellow Citron on a no. 8 flat, paint the green hulls at the tops of the berries. Pick up a little Wicker White to make the greens a bit more opaque.

7 To paint the blackberries, begin by basing in the round berries with Brilliant Blue on a no. 12 flat. Make the round shapes by painting two half circles.

8 Double load Brilliant Blue and Lavender on a no. 8 flat and begin painting the little round segments on each berry using little C-strokes. Begin on the outer edge and work toward the base.

9 Continue filling in the little C-stroke segments, picking up more Lavender on your brush as you go.

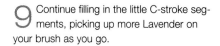

10 Paint little C-stroke segments on all the blackberries in your design, always keeping the Lavender side of the brush to the outside edge of each segment.

11 Finish the blackberries with the leaves, using a double load of Thicket and Yellow Citron on a no. 8 flat. If you need better coverage, pick up a little Wicker White on your brush to make the greens more opaque.

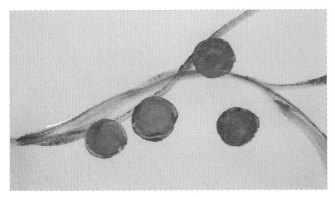

12 Begin painting the blueberries by basing in the round shapes with Brilliant Blue on no. 8 flat. Again, make two half circles with your brush to get a nice rounded berry shape.

13 Switch to a no. 6 flat and double load Wicker White and Lavender. Paint the blossom end with tiny ruffled five-petal flower shapes, varying the placement on each berry so the berries look like they're facing different directions along the vines.

14 Double load a no. 12 flat with Thicket and Yellow Citron, pick up a little Magenta. Paint the large leaves, keeping the Thicket to the outside. Vary your colors, some have lighter green to the outer edge, some have more magenta.

15 Add smaller leaves and some long, slender leaves among the larger ones. Pick up Asphaltum on the dirty brush and pull stems into all of the leaves.

16 Using a no. 8 flat and Inca Gold Metallic, paint the small one-stroke leaves and stems. Pick up Thicket and Yellow Citron on the gold brush to vary the colors for some of the leaves.

17 Using Metallic Pure Gold dimensional, outline and detail the leaves, add curls and tendrils, and pull stems into all the berries. Let all the paint dry completely before using your tablecloth.

elegant tablecloth

MATERIALS NEEDED

Colors: Metallic Solid Bronze, Metallic Inca Gold, Metallic Solid Bronze Dimensional.

Brushes: no. 16 flat, 5/8-inch (16mm) angular.

Surface: Ivory cotton-blend rectangular tablecloth from Target. Similar tablecloths are available at department or specialty stores. Wash and dry tablecloth before painting to remove sizing. Don't use liquid fabric softener or dryer sheets—this will prevent good adhesion of the paint.

Additional Supplies: Fabric Medium.

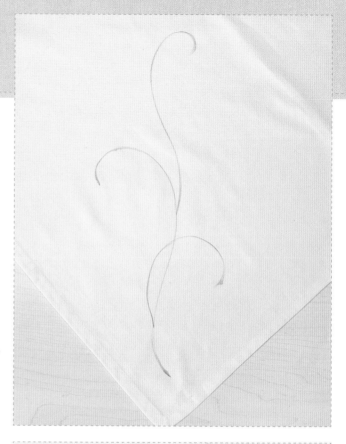

1 Begin your design in one corner of your rectangular tablecloth (this would also work well on a square tablecloth). Double load Metallic Solid Bronze and Metallic Inca Gold on a no. 16 flat and chisel edge the main stems for placement in the corner of the tablecloth. Pull these strokes away from the corner toward the center.

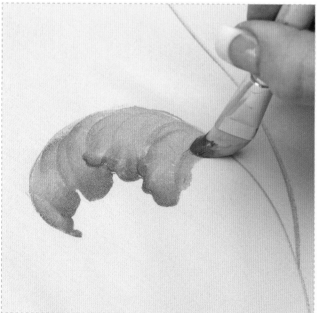

2 With the same brush and colors, begin painting the cupped acanthus leaf along one of the curving stems you just painted. Start at the stem, stroke outward in a curve, wiggle the brush to get the curly edge, then curve back to the stem. Keep the Bronze side of the brush to the outside edge of the leaf segments.

3 Continue painting the acanthus leaf, curving each stroke and nestling each leaf segment into the one before. As you near the base of the stem, make your strokes shorter and more tightly curved. On the final segment, pull a long tail that joins the stem.

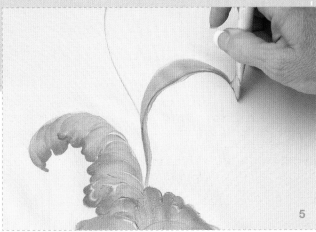

4 Add a large heart-shaped leaf next to the acanthus leaf, overlapping it along the stem side. Keep the Bronze side to the outside and paint the leaf with a very ruffled edge. Pull a chisel edge stem into it.

5 Paint the scrolls by starting on the chisel edge of the no. 16 flat where the two leaves meet, pressing down to widen the scroll in the middle, then lifting back up to the chisel and curving around. Don't turn or pivot your brush as you stroke.

6 With Metallic Solid Bronze on the 5/8-inch (16mm) angular brush, add long-tailed commas and smaller scrolls.

7 Outline the leaves and add details and curls using Metallic Solid Bronze dimensional.

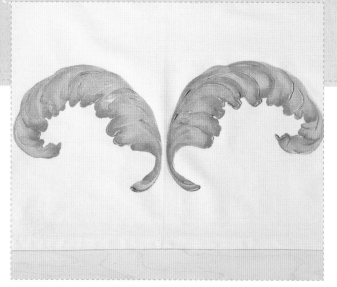

8 Along the shorter sides of the rectangular tablecloth, measure to find the center of the cloth. Make a light pencil mark there. Double load Metallic Solid Bronze and Metallic Inca Gold and place two curving, mirror-image lines for placement. Paint two cupped acanthus leaves that are mirror images of each other, following the instructions in steps 2 and 3 on page 88.

9 Add a couple of long and slender leaves coming up from the center. Paint some long-tailed commas using just the Metallic Solid Bronze on a 5/8-inch (16mm) angular brush, and add curls and tendrils with Metallic Solid Bronze dimensional, following the instructions in steps 6 and 7 on page 89.

10 On the long sides of the rectangular tablecloth, double load Metallic Solid Bronze and Metallic Inca Gold on a no. 16 flat. Paint the main placement vines to serve as your design template.

11 Along the leftmost line, paint a large cupped acanthus leaf just as you did in the corner of the cloth (see steps 2 and 3 on page 88).

12 Paint a couple of smaller, wiggle-edge leaves on each side of the main scrolls in the center. Pull chisel edge stems into them from the main scrolls.

13 Decorate the design with more scrolls, comma strokes and curled leaves as much as you wish.

14 Detail the leaves and add curls and tendrils with Metallic Solid Bronze dimensional. Let all the paint on the entire tablecloth dry completely before using.

floral napkins

MATERIALS NEEDED

Colors: Metallic Peridot and Metallic Peridot Dimensional, Glitter Blue Ocean Dimensional, Wicker White, Metallic Blue Topaz, Coastal Blue, Asphaltum.

Brushes: nos. 8, 12 and 16 flats, 1/2-inch (13mm) scruffy.

Surface: Four brown cotton-blend dinner napkins from Target. Similar items are available at department or specialty stores. Wash and dry napkins before painting to remove sizing. Don't use liquid fabric softener or dryer sheets—this will prevent good adhesion of the paint.

Additional Supplies: Fabric Medium.

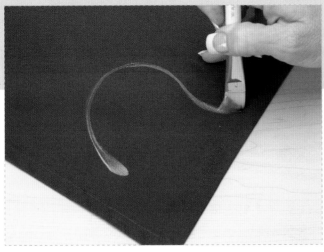

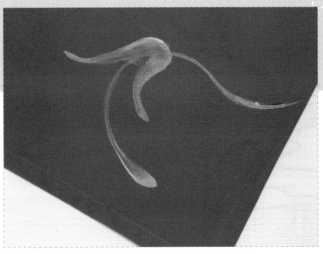

1 There are four different designs for this set of dinner napkins but since they all use the same colors, they will look fantastic on your dinner table. We'll start with the Green Tulip and Scrolls design shown on page 94. Load a no. 16 flat with Metallic Peridot and paint a comma stroke with a long, curving tail in one corner of the napkin.

2 With the same brush and color, paint the basic shape of the tulip halfway down the curving line you just painted.

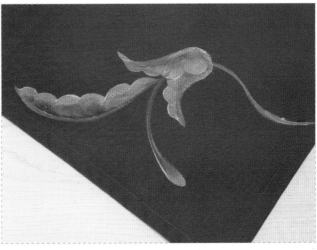

3 Paint scllops along the inner edges of the two tulip petals, overlapping the first one with the second petal at the base.

4 Paint a large curved leaf with a scalloped edge extending from the center of the tulip.

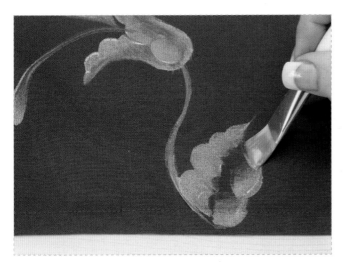

5 At the bottom of the long curving tail, paint a smaller leaf using segmented strokes.

6 Paint three long-tailed comma strokes coming out from the center of the tulip. With Metallic Peridot dimensional, outline the tulip and leaves and draw long curving curls and tendrils.

7 Using Glitter Blue Ocean dimensional, add a few blue glitter curls coming out of the tulip center and a series of tiny comma strokes on one of the tendrils. When this paint dries, you will see only the lines of deep turquoise glitter.

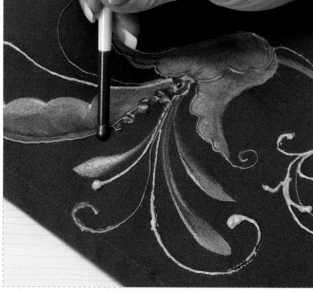

8 Add a touch of Wicker White to Metallic Blue Topaz and dot on blue berries with the tip end of the handle of the no. 16 flat brush. Follow the curving green stem of the large green leaf and let the berries diminish in size as you go up the stem. Let all the paint dry completely before using the napkin.

1 The design for the second napkin is a blue trumpet flower shown on page 96 (at left). Place in the stems with the chisel edge of a no. 8 flat and Metallic Peridot.

2 Draw the outline of the trumpet flower with Metallic Blue Topaz using the chisel edge of a no. 8 flat.

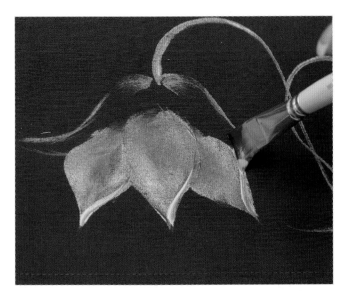

3 Switch to a no. 16 flat, double load Metallic Blue Topaz and Coastal Blue and paint all the back petals first, keeping the Metallic Blue Topaz to the outside. Outline the petals on one side with Coastal Blue.

4 With the same double loaded flat, paint the two front petals, then outline one edge of each petal with Coastal Blue and the other edge with Metallic Blue Topaz.

5 Double load a no. 16 flat with Metallic Peridot and Metallic Blue Topaz and paint a single-stroke ruffled-edge leaf, keeping the Peridot (green) side to the outside edges of the leaf.

6 Load a no. 12 flat with Metallic Peridot and paint little one-stroke leaves and stems coming off the main stems. Use Metallic Peridot dimensional to outline the large leaf, add tendrils and curls, and draw stamens and pollen dots in the tulip's center. Let all the paint dry completely before using the napkin.

1 The third napkin is painted with a blue tiger lily. Load a no. 8 flat with Metallic Peridot and draw the outlines of your leaves and a curving stem. Double load a no. 16 flat with Metallic Blue Topaz and Coastal Blue. With the lighter blue to the outside, outline the shapes of the petals, then fill them in.

2 Highlight and shade the petal edges with chisel edge strokes and Coastal Blue for the highlighted sides and Metallic Blue Topaz for the shaded sides. Pick up Metallic Peridot on the dirty brush and fill in the large leaves. Paint a C-stroke for the flower center.

3 To paint the spots on the petals of the tiger lily, load Asphaltum on a no. 8 flat and make short, parallel, chisel-edge strokes.

4 Using Metallic Peridot dimensional, finish with curls and tendrils extending from the leaves, and stamens coming out from the flower center. Add pollen dots at the ends of the stamens. Let all the paint dry completely before using the napkin.

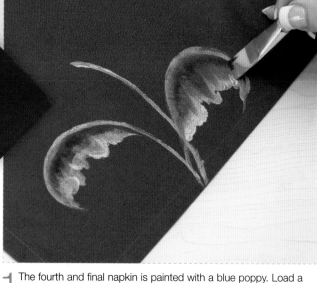

1 The fourth and final napkin is painted with a blue poppy. Load a no. 8 flat with Metallic Peridot and draw the upper curve of the leaves and a center stem. With a sideload float of Metallic Peridot on a no. 16 flat, pick up some Asphaltum on one side of brush and add the ruffly lower edge of the leaves.

2 Double load a no. 16 flat with Coastal Blue and Metallic Blue Topaz and paint the outer petal layer of the poppy blossom. Keep the Blue Topaz side of the brush to the outside edge of the petals.

3 Pick up more Coastal Blue on the dirty brush and paint the inner petals. Using Asphaltum on a 1/2-inch (13mm) scruffy, pounce in the brown center, then using the chisel edge of a no. 8 flat, pull streaks out onto the petals from the center. Using the Glitter Blue dimensional, add pollen dots in the center and outline the outer petals. The photo of the finished napkin at top left shows how the Glitter Blue dimensional looks when it is completely dry.

4 Using Metallic Peridot dimensional, finish with curls and tendrils extending from the leaves, and outline half of the flower center. Let all the paint dry completely before using the napkin.

chef's apron

MATERIALS NEEDED

Colors: Metallic Solid Bronze and Metallic Solid Bronze Dimensional, Asphaltum, Yellow Ochre, Thicket, Yellow Citron, Light Red Oxide, Engine Red, Berry Wine.

Brushes: nos. 12 and 16 flats.

Surface: Khaki cotton-blend chef's apron and striped towel from Sur la Table. Similar items are available at stores that sell cookware.

Additional Supplies: Fabric Medium.

1 Begin the fruit and leaves design by placing in the main branches and twigs. On this chef's apron, we'll place one grouping on the right side of the bib, and another one at the lower left extending onto the pocket of the apron. Double load Metallic Solid Bronze and Asphaltum on a no. 16 flat and use the chisel edge to draw the branches. Since they will be heavy with fruit, the branches should hang downward from the edges of the apron.

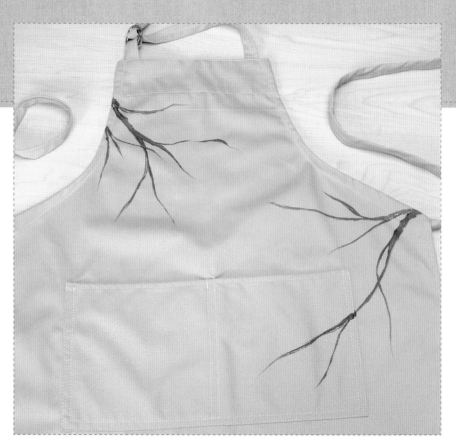

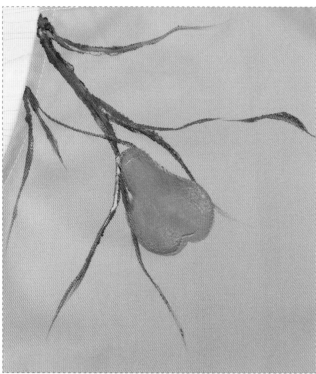

3 Add a second pear the same way, overlapping the first. With the dirty brush, sideload into Asphaltum and shade the same side of each pear. If your branch shows through your pear, re-stroke the branch on top of the pear. Pick up Thicket and Yellow Citron and tap in the bottom blossom ends of the pears.

2 Begin the pears using a no. 16 flat loaded with Yellow Ochre and sideloaded into Metallic Solid Bronze. Stroke the left half of the pear with the flat of the brush, keeping the Bronze to the outside and following the shape. Then reload the brush, flip it over and stroke in the other half of the pear. Re-stroke the center with Yellow Ochre to fill in if needed.

4 To begin the apples, double load Light Red Oxide and Engine Red on a no. 16 flat and sideload into Berry Wine. Stroke one half of the apple shape, keeping the Berry Wine to the outside edge of the apple.

5 Finish the other side of the apple, flipping the brush to put the Berry Wine on the outside edge. Fill in the center with Engine Red. Paint a second apple below the two pears the same way.

6 Pick up Yellow Ochre on the dirty brush and pull short curving strokes upward to highlight and round the apple.

7 To begin the leaves, using the dirty brush, pick up Thicket and Yellow Citron and pull a series of comma strokes for the first half of the large leaf that overlaps the pears.

8 Flip the brush over and paint the other half of the comma stroke leaf, keeping the Yellow Citron to the outside edge. Pull in a stem of Metallic Solid Bronze using the chisel edge of the flat.

10 Begin painting the green grapes with Metallic Solid Bronze and Yellow Citron double loaded on a no. 12 flat. Paint each grape with two half-circle strokes, with the Yellow Citron at the bottom and the Bronze at the top.

9 Overlap each apple with a large leaf using Thicket and Yellow Citron, picking up a little Engine Red for color. Fill in the design with some smaller one-stroke leaves and stems using the same colors as for the large leaves.

11 After all the green grapes are placed in, pick up Solid Bronze Metallic and Asphaltum on the dirty brush and pull little stems up from each grape using the chisel edge of the flat.

12 Finish by outlining the leaves and adding tendrils and curls using Metallic Solid Bronze dimensional. Let all the paint dry completely before using the apron.

The striped towel is painted with a cluster of green grapes, branches and stems, a large leaf and tendrils using the same colors as on the apron.

MATERIALS NEEDED

Colors: Fresh Foliage, Thicket, Coastal Blue, Wicker White, Yellow Light.

Brushes: no. 6 flat, no. 2 script liner.

Surface: White wicker basket with pink cotton canvas liner from Target. Similar items are available at home centers or specialty stores.

Additional Supplies: Fabric Medium.

1 Remove the liner from the basket and smooth it out for easier painting. With Fresh Foliage on a no. 2 script liner, paint the main vines and stems. Switch to a no. 6 flat and paint tiny one-stroke leaves and stems.

2 Double load the no. 6 flat with Fresh Foliage and Thicket and paint the dark green one-stroke leaves.

3 Load the no. 6 flat with Coastal Blue, sideload into Wicker White and paint the back wings of the blue butterfly.

4 The front wing is lower and the edge is scalloped. With the same brush and colors, outline the shape of the wing, then fill in the center. Load Thicket and Fresh Foliage on the no. 2 script liner and thin it with fabric medium. Paint the body of the butterfly and the antennae. Detail the wings with Yellow Light and Wicker White comma strokes.

5 With a no. 2 script liner, use inky Thicket to add the three-step curls coming off the main stems and vines. Let the paint dry completely before placing the liner back into the wicker basket.

monogrammed pillowcases

MATERIALS NEEDED

Colors: Wicker White and Wicker White Dimensional, Metallic Taupe, Asphaltum.

Brushes: nos. 12 and 16 flats.

Surface: Taupe cotton-blend pillowcases from Target. Similar items are available at department or specialty stores. Wash and dry pillowcases first before painting to remove sizing. Do not use liquid fabric softener or dryer sheets—this will prevent good adhesion of the paint.

Additional Supplies: Fabric Medium.

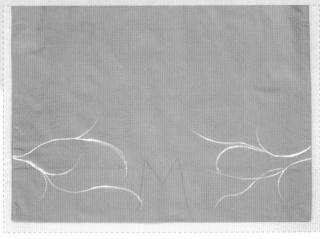

1 Pencil in the shape of the monogram letter in the center of the pillowcase's open edge. (You can download many different lettering styles from the internet or use a lettering stencil.) Use a no. 12 flat and inky Wicker White (use fabric medium to thin it, not water) and place in the main stems to lay out your design.

2 Double load Metallic Taupe and Wicker White on a no. 16 flat. Keeping the Wicker White to the outer edge, begin painting one half of the large maple leaf. Stroke each lobe of the leaf separately. Continue picking up Wicker White on your brush as you stroke.

3 Paint the other half of the maple leaf the same way. Be sure to flip your brush so the Wicker White is always to the outside edge of the leaf.

4 As you paint each lobe of the leaf, pull your stroke back to the center before beginning the next lobe.

5 The final lobes should become shorter as they approach the outer tip of the leaf. The final one should come to a point. Pick up Wicker White on the brush and chisel-edge a stem coming partway into the center of the leaf.

6 Moving inward along the stem toward the center of the pillow-case, the next leaf is a side view leaf. Double load Metallic Taupe and Wicker White on a no. 16 flat. Stroke out and pull back to the main curving stem. The lobes get progressively larger, then smaller again as you get to the outer tip.

7 Finish up by stroking a long curving line to clean up the center vein.

8 The next leaf is a two-layer folded leaf at the outer edge of the pillowcase. Using the same brush and colors, stroke three large lobes for the back half of the leaf.

9 Pick up lots more Wicker White on the brush and paint the front half of the leaf, making these lobes shorter and lighter.

10 With Wicker White dimensional, out-line and detail the leaves and add curls and tendrils all over the design. Repeat steps 2 through 10 on the other side of the pillowcase to create a mirror image of this side.

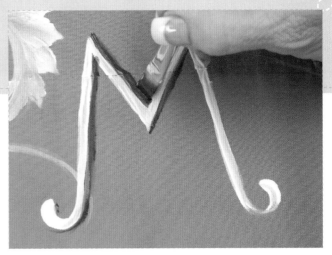

11 Load a no. 12 flat with Wicker White and stroke the shape of the monogram. Don't worry that the lines are not smooth—we'll fix that with the shading in the next step.

12 Thin Asphaltum with fabric medium and shade the monogram by staying up on the chisel edge of the brush and stroking along only the right side of each part of the white monogram. Let all the paint dry completely before using the pillowcases.

satin bathrobe

MATERIALS NEEDED

Colors: Lavender, Wicker White, Metallic Amethyst, Orchid, Metallic Peridot and Metallic Peridot Dimensional.

Brush: no. 8 flat.

Surface: White satin bathrobe by Flora Nikrooz from Macy's. Similar items are available in the fine lingerie or sleepwear sections at any department store.

Additional Supplies: Fabric Medium.

1 Double load Lavender and Wicker White on a no. 8 flat and start the first layer of hydrangea florets. Keep the Lavender side of the brush to the outside of each petal. Make some of the florets fully open, some sideview, some partial and overlap them as you fill in.

2 Pick up Metallic Amethyst on the dirty brush and paint a few darker florets here and there. Add some single trailing petals at the bottom of the cluster.

3 Double load Orchid and Wicker White on a no. 8 flat and paint some pink florets to help enrich the colors and round out the hydrangea blossom. Stroke a couple of pink trailing petals too.

4

5

4 Double load Metallic Peridot and Wicker White on a no. 8 flat and paint some large, heart-shaped leaves tucked in around the hydrangea, plus some smaller one-stroke leaves. Pull some chisel-edge stems partway into the larger leaves.

5 With the same brush and colors, pull some long-tailed comma strokes starting outside the flower cluster and pulling toward it with a push-and-lift stroke. Use the Metallic Peridot dimensional to dot in the hydrangea centers.

parson's chair cover

MATERIALS NEEDED

Colors: Asphaltum, Wicker White, Metallic Amethyst, Thicket, Metallic Peridot Dimensional, Yellow Ochre, Metallic Pure Gold Dimensional.

Brushes: nos. 8 and 12 flats, 5/8-inch (16mm) angular, no. 2 script liner.

Surface: Sage green cotton-poly chair cover from Target. Similar chair covers are available at department and specialty stores.

Additional Supplies: Fabric Medium.

1 Double load Asphaltum and a little Wicker White on a 5/8-inch (16mm) angular brush and place in the main stems using the chisel edge of the brush. Start at the center bottom of the chair cover and pull the stems upward and outward.

2 Pick up Metallic Amethyst and some fabric medium on the dirty brush and paint the pale purple shadow ferns. Load Thicket and fabric medium on the same brush and paint the green shadow ferns.

3 Load a no. 12 flat with Metallic Amethyst and paint the purple lupines. Every once in a while, pick up a touch of Wicker White to provide color variation in the petals. Stroke each petal separately and start at the bottom of the cone-shaped blossom, working up to the tip.

4 The darkest green ferns are painted with a brush mix of Thicket and Asphaltum plus a bit of fabric medium, using a no. 12 flat. Since these ferns are darker and stand out more, paint the leaves carefully and neatly. Overlap the purple lupine with a few of the leaves. Then pull a center stem up the middle of each fern frond.

5 Add some green tendrils and curlicues to fill in your design, using Metallic Peridot dimensional. These are very freeform so work quickly and squeeze the bottle consistently for smooth and graceful lines.

6 To paint the butterfly, double load Yellow Ochre and Wicker White on a no. 8 flat and pick up a little Asphaltum on the Yellow Ochre side. Paint the back wing first, keeping the dark side of the brush to the outside edge of the wing.

7 Paint the front wings next using the same brush and colors. Pick up more Wicker White on your brush to provide contrast between the back wing and the front.

8 Load a no. 2 script liner with Asphaltum and paint the body and antennae. Use Metallic Pure Gold dimensional to outline the body, dot the antenna tips, and detail the spots on the wings.

bath towels

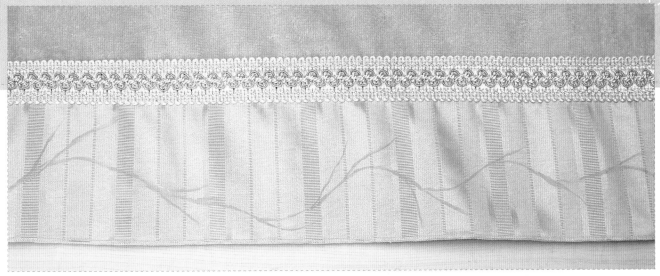

1 When painting on bath towels, look for a style that has a wide border sewn onto one end. This towel has a smooth satiny border material with just a little bit of texture in the stripes—perfect for painting an elegant rose and leaves design. Double load Wicker White and Metallic Rose Shimmer on a no. 12 flat. Pick up a tiny bit of Lemon Custard to warm up the color. Start with the curving main vine and stems, using the chisel edge of the brush.

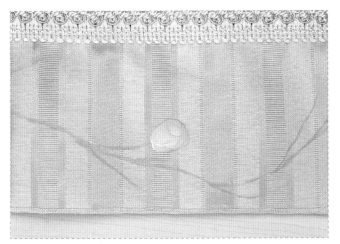

2 Begin the large rose in the center of the design by basing in the center bud of the rose blossom. The back of the bud is a C-stroke and the front is a U stroke. Keep the pink side of the brush to the top.

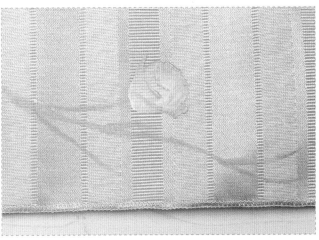

3 Pull a couple of petals from each side across the front of the bud to begin building the layers.

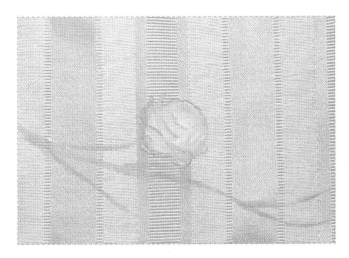

4 Pick up more Rose Shimmer Metallic on the brush and add a couple of curled-edge petals at the base of the center bud.

5 Double load a no. 12 flat with Wicker White and Metallic Rose Shimmer. Begin adding a few closed rosebuds on both sides of the main rose, starting with the center bud just as you did in step 2. For the small side petals, pick up more Wicker White on your brush.

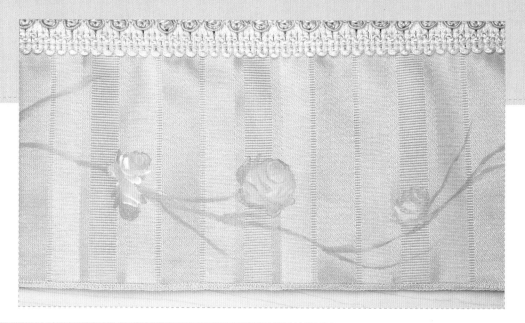

6 Load a no. 12 flat with Metallic Rose Shimmer and paint the rose leaves. Stroke up to the tip, wiggling the brush slightly to get a serrated edge, then wiggle back to the base. These leaves are painted in pairs opposite each other on the stems.

7 Fill in along the main vine with more Rose Shimmer Metallic leaves. Pick up a little Wicker White sometimes for color variations. As the design moves away from the center of the border, the leaves and roses should become sparser.

8 If you wish, define and embellish the rose petals and leaves using Pearl Champagne dimensional paint. Use the tip to loosely outline the leaves and indicate the petal edges. Be sure to let all the paint dry completely before using your towels.

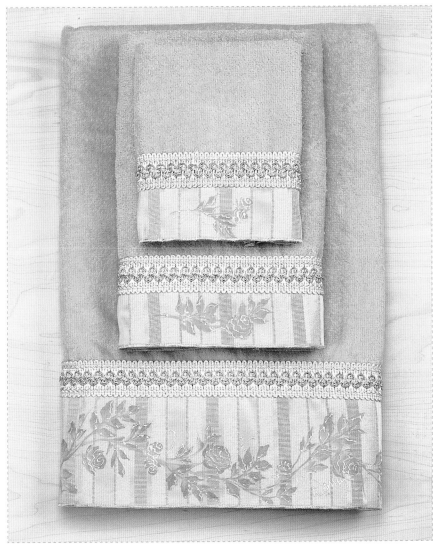

quilted throw

MATERIALS NEEDED

Colors: Yellow Ochre, Wicker White and Wicker White Dimensional, Metallic Peridot and Metallic Peridot Dimensional, Hauser Green Medium.

Brushes: nos. 6, 12 and 16 flats, no. 2 script liner.

Surface: Quilted throw blanket with polyester fill, from Linens 'N' Things. Similar throws are available at home and department stores.

Additional Supplies: Fabric Medium.

1 The first design is a large, five-petal flower. Double load Yellow Ochre and Wicker White on a no. 16 flat and paint the five large ruffled petals.

2 Double load Metallic Peridot and Hauser Green Medium on a no. 12 flat and add a few leaves.

3 Loosely outline the ruffly petals with Wicker White dimensional and add details to the flower's center. Outline and detail the green leaves with Metallic Peridot dimensional.

4 The second design is an ethereal white dragonfly. Double load Yellow Ochre and Wicker White on a no. 16 flat and paint the dragonfly wings. The upper two are larger and longer than the lower two.

5 Paint the dragonfly's body with Metallic Peridot and Hauser Green Medium double loaded on a no. 6 flat. The green antennae are done with a no. 2 script liner. Sideload into Wicker White and indicate the body segments with little C-strokes.

6 With Wicker White dimensional paint, use the tip of the bottle to loosely outline the wings. Detail the body with a wavy line of Metallic Peridot dimensional, and add dots on the tips of the antennae.

7 The third design on the quilted throw is a lacy fern. Double load Hauser Green Medium and Metallic Peridot on a no. 12 flat. Place the stems of the fern. Pick up Wicker White on the same brush and begin painting the little chisel-edge fern leaves. Start at the outer tip of each stem and work your way downward toward the main stem.

8 Fill in with more chisel-edge fern leaves along the stems, re-loading the brush every few strokes with the two greens, and picking up Wicker White occasionally.

9 With Wicker White dimensional paint, use the tip of the bottle to detail the fern with short highlight lines on each leaf.

10 The fourth design is a yellow lily. Double load Yellow Ochre and Wicker White on a no. 16 flat. For each of the large pointed petals, begin at the base, slide up to the tip, and slide back down to the base. Keep the Yellow Ochre side of the brush to the outside edge of the petals.

11 Paint a total of six long pointed petals to complete the lily. Make sure the base of each petal begins in the center of the flower. If needed, turn your surface to make painting easier.

12 Loosely outline the lily petals with lines of Wicker White dimensional, extending the petal tips and giving each one a little curl at the end. Pull long, curving stamens with Metallic Peridot dimensional, and indicate the center with short curving strokes.

13 The fifth design is a white hydrangea blossom. Start by painting a large hydrangea leaf using Metallic Peridot and Wicker White double loaded on a large flat brush. Keep the Peridot to the outside edge.

14 Double load a no. 12 flat with Yellow Ochre and Wicker White. Begin the individual florets. Each floret has four or five petals, with the white side of the brush always to the outside edge of each petal.

15 Fill in with more florets until the hydrangea looks full and rounded, overlapping some of the florets and painting a few partial ones along the outside edge.

16 Detail the florets with Wicker White dimensional, using the tip of the bottle to draw loose outlines and dot in the centers. With Metallic Peridot dimensional, outline and detail the green leaf.

17 The sixth and final design is a simple yellow daisy. Double load Yellow Ochre and Wicker White on a no. 16 flat and paint a circle of long, slender, yellow daisy petals. Pull each petal from the outer tip in toward the center. Turn your surface to make painting the petals easier.

18 Pick up more Wicker White on the dirty brush and add another layer of lighter yellow petals in between the darker yellow ones. With Wicker White dimensional paint, use the tip of the bottle to loosely outline the edges of each petal and dot in the center. With Metallic Peridot dimensional, make a circle of green dots around the white ones to define the daisy's center.

Because this throw is quilted into large squares, I placed my six designs in one corner, with one design per square. I repeated them on the opposite corner so the throw would look nice from any direction.

resources

index

U.S. RETAILERS

Paints, Brushes & Supplies

Dewberry Designs, Inc.
355 Citrus Tower Blvd., Suite 104
Clermont, FL 34711
Ph. (352) 394-7344
www.onestroke.com

Plaid Enterprises, Inc.
3225 Westech Dr.
Norcross, GA 30092
Ph. (800) 842-4197
www.plaidonline.com

Electric Applicator for Crystals

BeJeweler®Pro Next Generation
Precision Electric Rhinestone Applicator
for Hot-Fix Embellishments

Creative Crystal Company
Sarasota, FL
Ph. 1-800-578-0716
www.creativecrystal.com

Pre-glued Crystals

Swarovski® Hot-Fix Rhinestones

Creative Crystal Company
Sarasota, FL
Ph. 1-800-578-0716
www.creativecrystal.com

Ultrafine Art Glitter

"Barnyard" Kit of 6 Colors
and Adhesive

Art Institute Glitter
712 N. Balboa St.
Cottonwood, AZ 86326
Ph. (928) 639-0805
www.artglitter.com

CANADIAN RETAILERS

Crafts Canada
120 North Archibald St.
Thunder Bay, ON P7C 3X8
Tel: 888-482-5978
www.craftscanada.ca

Folk Art Enterprises
P.O. Box 1088
Ridgetown, ON, N0P 2C0
Tel: 800-265-9434

MacPherson Arts & Crafts
91 Queen St. E., P.O. Box 1810
St. Mary's, ON, N4X 1C2
Tel: 800-238-6663
www.macphersoncrafts.com

Acrylic paints, 8
Acrylic wrap, 55-56
Apples, 101
Applicator, electric, for crystals, 9, 21
Apron, 99-103

Baby bloomers, 74-75
Bathrobe, satin, 110-112
Bath towels, 116-119
Berries, 81, 83-85, 94
Bibs, 71-73
Blackberries, 84-85
Blueberries, 85
Branches and twigs, 100
Brushes, 8
  double loading, 12
  multi-loading, 13
Brushstrokes, 16-19
  half-circle, 102
  push-and-lift, 112
  serrated-tip petal, 19, 28, 32, 118
  teardrop, 79
  touch-and-pull, 34
  See also Comma strokes, C-strokes, One-stroke leaves
Butterflies, 32, 48-49, 72, 105, 115

Cabbage rose, 63-64
Camisole, sparkly, 44-45
Canvas basket liner, 104-105
Chair cover, 113-115
Christening gown, 66-68
Comma strokes, 34, 58, 105
  clusters, 51
  large, 25
  large and small, 56
  long-tailed, 17, 63, 89-90, 93, 112
Cotton-blend fabrics
  apron and dishtowel, 99-103
  napkins, 92-98
  pillowcases, 106-109
  tablecloth, 82-86, 87-91
Cotton fabrics
  baby bloomers, 74-75
  bibs, 71-73
  christening gown, 66-68
  shirt, 40-41
Cotton/spandex camisole, 44-45
Crystals
  applying, 11, 21, 29, 43, 45, 47, 51, 56
  electric applicator for, 9, 21

C-strokes, 61, 84-85, 97, 121
Cupped acanthus leaf, 18
Curlicues, 54, 56, 59, 115
Curls, 51, 90-91, 94, 96, 97, 98,
    103, 105, 108
    two-step, 17

Daisies, 29, 75, 125
Denim jacket, 38-39
Dimensional paints, 11, 14-15,
    41, 51
    curls, 65
    "squeeze-release" motion, 54
    applying smoothly, 115
    curls and tendrils, 94
    dotting, 43
    outlining and detailing, 86
Dish towels, 80-81, 99, 103
Double loading, 12
Double Loading Carousel, 9
Dragonflies, 73, 121
Dry-brushing, 51

Edges
    curly, 88
    folded, 28
    lacy, 41
    ruffled, 16, 35-36, 43, 59, 89,
        96, 98
    scalloped, 51, 53, 93
    wiggle, 91
    wiggle and smooth, 81

Fabric
    bleeding through, 23
    new, method for washing, 23
Fabric medium, 12, 23
Fabric softener, avoiding, 23
Ferns, 77, 114, 122
Flowers, 58-59
    daisies, 29, 75, 125
    five-petal, 41, 54, 56, 85, 121.
        See also Violets
    fuchsia, 31-32
    gold and silver, 47
    hydrangeas, 111-112, 124
    large pink, 43
    lilies, 28, 97-98, 123
    lupines, 114
    morning glories, 53
    poppy, 98
    roses, 61-65, 117-118
    stylized, 34-37
    trumpet, 95-96
    tulip, 93-94

violets, 67
Frame, 61
Fruit
    apples, 101
    berries, 81 94
    blackberries, 84-85
    blueberries, 85
    grapes, 102-103
    pears, 100
    strawberries, 83

Glitter, ultrafine art, 11
    applying, 20, 45, 56
Grapes, 102-103
Grapevine, 83

Half-circle strokes, 102
Handbag. *See* Purse
Hydrangeas, 124

Jacket
    denim, 38-39
    linen, 27-29
Jeans, 24-26

Lacy effects, 15, 26
Laptop computer bag, 57-59
Leaf segments, defined, 36
Leaf with scrolls, 24-26
Leaves, 16-19
    acanthus, 18, 59, 88, 90
    blueberry, 85
    comma stroke, 102
    curled, 36
    drooping, 65
    heart-shaped, 89, 112
    hydrangea, 124
    large, 97
    long and slender, 31, 53
    maple, 107
    ruffled-edge, 98
    side view, 108
    single-stroke ruffled-edge, 96
    two-layer folded, 108
    two-stroke, 77, 81
    variety, 59
    varying color, 63
    varying shape, 78
    wiggle-edge, 58, 91
    See also Ferns, One-stroke
        leaves
Lilies, 28-29, 123
Linen blend skirt, 42-43
Linen jacket, 27-29
Liner, wicker basket, 104-105

Lines, cleaning up, 15
Lupines, 114

Mistakes, fixing, 15
Monogram letter, 107, 109
Morning glories, 53
Multi-loading, 13

Napkins, floral, 92-98

One-stroke leaves, 16, 37, 41, 47,
    51, 56, 58, 61, 65, 75, 86, 96,
    105
One-stroke painting, 12-19
Outlining, 15, 26, 39, 41, 43, 79,
    86, 89, 94, 96, 103, 108
    flowers, 29
    loosely, 119, 121, 123, 125

Paints
    acrylic, 8
    dimensional, 14-15
    dimensional glitter, 11, 20, 23
Paisley, 43
Pants
    black, 33-37
    See also Jeans
Peacock feather, 79
Pears, 100
Petals. *See* Flowers
Photo album, 62-65
Pillows
    decorative, 76-79
    ringbearer's, 69-70
Pillowcases, 106-109
Pods, 35
Poppy, 98
Pot holders, 80-81
Purse
    casual, 52-54
    dressy, 50-51
Push-and-lift stroke, 112

Quilted throw, 120-125

Ribbon, 61
Rose leaves, 18
Roses, 61, 63-65, 117-118
Ruffled-edge leaves, 16. *See also*
    Edges, ruffled

Satin fabrics
    ballet flats, 46-47
    bathrobe, 110-112
    purse, 50-51

ringbearer's pillow, 69-70
Scallop-edged leaf, 19, 51, 93
Scroll design, 25, 51, 70, 89, 91
Scrolling leaves, 17
Shading, 53-54, 100, 109
Shawl. *See* Wrap, elegant
Shell stroke, segmented, 19
Shirt, tailored, 40-41
Shirt form, 9
    for camisole, 45
    for cotton shirt, 41
    for jacket, 28
    for tee shirt, 31
Shoes, satin ballet flats, 46-47
Silk, decorative pillows, 76-79
Skirt, linen a-line, 42-43
Socks, butterfly, 449
Stems
    chisel-edge, 88, 95, 102-103,
        112, 114
    curving, 88
    and tendrils, 47
    See also Vines and stems
Strawberries, 83
Stripes, 61
Sunflower, sparkly, 44-45

Tablecloths
    elegant, 87-91
    kitchen, 82-86
Teardrop stroke, 58, 79
Tee shirt, watercolor, 30-31
Tendrils, 37, 47, 54, 56, 59, 90, 94,
    96, 97, 98, 103, 108, 115
Tiger lily, 97-98
Touch and pull strokes, 34
Tulips, 39, 93-94

Vines, 90
    and stems, 31, 34, 53, 105, 117
    See also Grapevine
Violets, 67

Waffle-weave towels, 80-81
Watercolor, creating in spray bottle,
    31
Wedding album, 60-61
Wet-into-wet, 23
Wings
    butterfly, 72
    dragonfly, 73
Wrap, elegant, 55-56

The best in decorative painting instruction is from North Light Books!

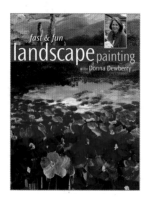

Fast & Fun Landscape Painting with Donna Dewberry

Learn to paint gorgeous landscapes the One-Stroke way! In this inspiring guide, beloved artist and PBS painting instructor Donna Dewberry shows you how easy and fun it is to paint a range of enchanting outdoor scenes using her popular One-Stroke painting techniques. From peaceful sunsets and breathtaking vistas to flowered fields and blooming gardens, Donna makes every painting achievable and satisfying. You'll find 15 complete start-to-finish landscape painting demonstrations, 27 quick demos on how to paint those details that make your landscape paintings pop, plus 15 handy tear-out cards featuring all of Donna's paint colors. Best of all, most paintings can be completed in an afternoon or less, thanks to Donna's clever sponging and brush-loading techniques. What could be more fun?
ISBN-13: 978-1-60061-025-7, ISBN-10: 1-60061-025-0, paperback, 144 pages, #Z1309

Gorgeous Glass: 20 sparkling ideas for painting on glass and china

Painting on glass and china is fun, easy and a creative way to bring the latest designer looks to your home! Twenty colorful and sparkling projects show you, step by step, how to paint designer-quality table settings, wedding gifts and home decor. From simple to sophisticated, classic to contemporary, elegant or natural, you'll find dozens of great ideas and designs, including reverse-painted bamboo plates and matching teapot, delicate bridal lace crystal champagne flutes, flowering herbs painted on tile coasters, traditional French country stemware, and so much more. Hundreds of full-color photos guide you through the simple steps to dazzling results!
ISBN-13: 978-1-60061-006-6, ISBN-10: 1-60061-006-4, paperback, 128 pages, #Z1002

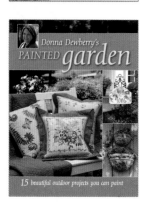

Donna Dewberry's Painted Garden

Beautify your outdoor decor with Donna Dewberry! See how easy it is to transform ordinary outdoor furniture and accessories into unique decorative objects using Donna's popular One-Stroke painting technique. With hundreds of colorful step-by-step photos, you'll learn how to paint 37 all-new projects, from wooden planters and glass candle-holders to metal wind chimes, an outdoor clock and so much more. The paints are durable and weatherproof and the projects are fun to do, even for complete beginners!
ISBN-13: 978-1-58180-949-7, ISBN-10: 1-58180-949-2, paperback, 128 pages, #Z0658

Sponge Painting: Fast & fun techniques for creating beautiful art

Want to paint gorgeous florals and dramatic landscapes on canvas in less than three hours? Professional artist Terrence Tse shows you how to put all the joy back into painting with his fun and unique sponge-painting techniques. His secret? He uses regular acrylic paints and a common household sponge! In this full-color, step-by-step book, you can choose from 20 start-to-finish painting demonstrations and create your own masterpiece in as little as 90 minutes. You'll learn how to use a sponge to paint everything from orchids, lilies and tulips to palm trees, bamboo and cherry blossoms; from moonlit lakes and reflective rivers to poppy-strewn fields, misty mountains and an early morning sunrise. No brushes—and no experience—needed!
ISBN-13: 978-1-58180-962-6, ISBN-10: 1-58180-962-X, paperback, 128 pages, #Z0686

These books and other fine North Light titles are available at your local art or craft retailer, bookstore or online supplier, or visit our website at www.mycraftivity.com.